What People Are Saying about
The Soul of a Leader

"*The Soul of a Leader* **breaks the mold of leadership books.** Both practical and inspiring, Margaret Benefiel's book lays out a path we can follow to make a real difference in whatever world we land. Benefiel helps me to dare to dream, battle for my soul, and break through the barriers that keep me from succeeding."

— David Batstone, professor and author,
Saving the Corporate Soul and *Not For Sale*

"Today's global community desperately needs leaders with soul. Margaret Benefiel's **groundbreaking book** meets that need beautifully, by teaching principles of soulful leadership, illustrated with stories of real leaders who practice them. Required reading."

— Archbishop Desmond Tutu, Nobel Peace Prize Winner

"*The Soul of a Leader* **touched the soul of this reader.** With her stories of real people struggling to lead with soul in a variety of workplaces, Margaret Benefiel guides others through the important steps of becoming a soulful leader. She does not minimize the difficulties, but makes the journey possible for all committed to this path."

— Rev. Jane E. Vennard, author, *A Praying Congregation:*
The Art of Teaching Spiritual Practice

"No organizational leaders reading this book can help but find both inspiration and practical, concrete help for nurturing their own souls and the soul of their organization. The author's deep organizational and spiritual background **provides a realistic yet visionary ground** for attending the inner life of leaders and the workers of their organizations, in close relation to the practical outer needs of organizational life. The book paves the way for soul-full personal and organizational life that brings the fruits of integrity, shared values, mutual respect, and success, illustrated through many inspiring stories of leaders and the transformation of their organizations."

— Rev. Dr. Tilden Edwards, Founder and Senior Fellow, Shalem Institute for Spiritual Formation

"Margaret Benefiel has gone right to the source — leaders who have chosen a deeper, more soulful path to building better organizations and a better society. Their stories are woven together to provide **inspiring lessons for all of us** who seek to build depth and spirit at work."

— Lee Bolman, professor and author, *Leading with Soul*

"**This book is a must read** for all those who ever considered grounding their lives and work in love and service to pursue a higher calling that just might change the world. Margaret Benefiel is one of the most creative thinkers on spiritual leadership alive today, and *The Soul of a Leader* is an accessible taste of her brilliance. Like a masterful conductor, she combines theology with science and presents a practical guide filled with case studies and everyday examples that we can all follow in our own spiritual journey."

— Louis W. (Jody) Fry, Professor of Management, Tarleton State University – Central Texas

"For the new generation of leaders who are replacing the Baby Boomers, **please read this engaging book** so you can take over leadership with soul and spirit and heart! Margaret gives you real-life examples and practical steps to take in your own setting and create the kind of organization you envision!"

— Charlotte Roberts, coauthor of the million-selling *The Fifth Discipline Fieldbook*

"Margaret Benefiel has written a book that is **powerfully inspirational and eminently practical.** Through the use of stories culled from interviews with leaders with soul, she provides excellent guidance as to how to lead with soul."
                                         — Jerry Biberman, editor,
                    Journal of Management, Spirituality, and Religion

"Benefiel's gentle yet incisive insights remind us all that leadership at its core is grounded in the soul. Her collection of human stories illustrate various themes that will help leaders nourish their souls and strengthen their leadership."
                    — David W. Miller, Ph.D., author, *God at Work,*
                                        resident, the Avodah Institute

"**In the tradition of Peter Block's** *Stewardship* **and Robert Greenleaf's** *On Becoming a Servant Leader,* Margaret Benefiel's *The Soul of a Leader* takes us on a journey into the qualities of knowing and action that are necessary for leading a soulful organization. She does so with stories and images of men and women who made hard choices and difficult decisions, guided by their inner moral compass and a higher purpose. The book tackles subjects that will be welcome by everyone who wishes to make a leadership contribution. The book includes topics such as keeping people first, the power of gratitude, and the need to break cycles of violence that limit our organizational and communal potential. **A wonderful book.**"
                    — Alan Briskin, author, *The Stirring of Soul in the Workplace,*
          and co-author of *Bringing Your Soul to Work* and *Daily Miracles*

"Something is changing dramatically in the world of organizational leadership. No longer is it just enough to meet quarterly expectations and grow the bottom line. Leaders themselves are finding their soul and wanting to grow spiritually in a way that is integrated with their work and family life. And as they grow personally, they begin to feel called to nurture the soul formation of those who work with them in the organizations they lead. **Margaret's Benefiel's brilliant book** *The Soul of a Leader* provides an inspirational and practical guide to leading with soul. This will become an important reference book for those pioneers who are leading from the deepest core of who they are, and who are committed to making a positive difference in the world."

— Judi Neal, Ph.D., President & CEO, International Center for Spirit at Work; author of *Edgewalkers: People and Organizations That Take Risks, Build Bridges, and Break New Ground*

"Leadership that matters inevitably requires focus, resilience, commitment, compassion, imagination, and a high tolerance of risk — all dependent upon a strength and competence of soul. Benefiel's understanding of the path of the soul — the quagmires, resources, and triumphs — is grounded, credible, and evocative. **This book is worth your time.**"

— Sharon Daloz Parks, author of *Leadership Can Be Taught: A Bold Approach for a Complex World*

THE SOUL
OF A
LEADER

About the Author

Margaret Benefiel, Ph.D., is CEO of ExecutiveSoul.com and author of the bestselling *Soul at Work: Spiritual Leadership in Organizations.* She also teaches at Andover Newton Theological School in Boston, in the area of spirituality and organizational leadership. For the 2003–2004 academic year, she occupied the O'Donnell Chair of Spirituality at the Milltown Institute in Dublin, Ireland.

She speaks widely, leads seminars and retreats, and offers coaching and spiritual direction to executives and organizations. She is a member of the Academy of Management, the Organizational Behavior Teaching Society, the American Academy of Religion, and Spiritual Directors International. She serves as Chair-Elect of the Academy of Management's Management, Spirituality, and Religion Group and has served on the governing board of the Society for the Study of Christian Spirituality.

A member of the Beacon Hills Friends Meeting, she lives in Boston with her husband.

THE SOUL
OF A
LEADER

Finding Your Path to
Fulfillment and Success

MARGARET BENEFIEL

A Crossroad Book
The Crossroad Publishing Company
New York

The author thanks:
The editors of the *Leadership Quarterly* for permission to use selected passages that origi-
nally appeared in different form in "The Second Half of the Journey: Spiritual Leadership for
Organizational Transformation," *Leadership Quarterly* 16, no. 5 (2005).

The editors of *Radical Grace* for permission to use selected passages that originally appeared in
"Humility, Confession and Customer Service," *Radical Grace* 20, no. 4 (2007).

The editors of *Spirituality and Business: Theory, Practice, and Future Directions* for permission to
use selected passages that originally appeared in "Deep Knowledge for Transformative Action:
The Use of Action Research in MSR," *Spirituality and Business: Theory, Practice, and Future
Directions,* ed. Jerry Biberman and Len Tischler (New York: Palgrave Macmillan, 2008).

Individuals portrayed in this book have consented to being quoted and named. They do not
necessarily represent the views of the institutions with which they are affiliated.

The Crossroad Publishing Company
16 Penn Plaza – 481 Eighth Avenue, Suite 1550
New York, NY 10001

Printed in the United States of America

The text of this book is set in 11/14 AGaramond. The display face is Univers.

Library of Congress Cataloging-in-Publication Data

Benefiel, Margaret.
    Soul of a leader : finding your path to fulfillment and success / Margaret
Benefiel.
        p. cm.
    ISBN-13: 978-0-8245-2480-7 (alk. paper)
    ISBN-10: 0-8245-2480-2 (alk. paper)
    1. Leadership. I. Title.
HD57.7.B4574 2008
658.4'092 – dc22

                                                            2008028227

1   2   3   4   5   6   7   8   9   10   12   11   10   09   08

CONTENTS

PART TWO
STAYING ON TRACK

PART THREE
PERSEVERING TO THE END

ACKNOWLEDGMENTS

First and foremost, I want to thank the many leaders who opened their hearts, minds, and lives to me in so generously consenting to be interviewed for this book. You provided me with a window into your souls, inspired me with your vision and dedication, and made this book possible.

I am grateful to John Jones and Roy Carlisle, editors at Crossroad Publishing Company, who, from the moment I met them at the American Academy of Religion annual meeting in Washington, D.C., believed in me. You envisioned this book and inspired me to write it; thank you for giving me the push and direction that I needed. And to John Jones, editor extraordinaire, my heartfelt thanks for walking with me each step of the way. Not only were you an excellent editor, but you also knew exactly when and how to encourage me. I felt affirmed by you in crucial moments along the way when my zeal would have otherwise flagged. To the entire team at Crossroad, especially Nancy Neal, Linabel Herrera, and John Eagleson, my deep gratitude. Your enthusiasm for and careful attention to this project made it a delight to work with you. I am also grateful to my agent, Sheryl Fullerton, who believed in me and helped me envision the possibilities for this book. Thank you for being a good friend as well as a competent and effective agent.

Eastern Point Retreat House in Gloucester, Massachusetts, provided a prayerful, inspiring atmosphere and excellent spiritual direction for writing retreats at three critical stages of the book. In addition, my friends generously prayed for and encouraged me, bearing with me as I wrestled with my demons and responding lovingly to my e-mail updates. Friends and family who read drafts offered many helpful suggestions and gave me fresh perspective: my deep thanks to Sue Lewis Bodner, Beth Bowden, Bill Dietrich, Joyce Gibson, Marilyn Greenberg, Ken Haase, Kay Hall, Deb Heau, Tom Henry, W. G. Henry, Keith Hwang, Debora Jackson, Kathy Koplik, Judy Locke, Monica Manning, Chuck McCorkle, Carol Mitchell, Linda Triemstra, Bob Ward, Rita Weathersby, and Penny Yunuba. Friends with whom I shared contemplative writing days helped me stay spiritually grounded and encouraged tender shoots of this book as they emerged: my thanks to Susie Allen, Andrea Bliss-Lerman, Monica Manning, Faith Ngunjiri, Beckey Phipps, Judy Proctor, Mary Shotwell, and Cathy Whitmire. My wonderful assistant Lisa Zeidenberg provided excellent transcripts of interviews and careful, inspired editing of chapters. To each and every one of you, thank you so very much.

Last but certainly not least, I want to thank my family. My mother, Willa Jones, who always believed in me and encouraged my projects, died suddenly at an early stage of this project, and I felt her loss deeply. My father, Wes Benefiel, showed interest and pride all along the way and kept me encouraged. My sisters, Beth Bowden and Virginia Buck, prayed for me and supported me. My aunts and cousins kept inquiring about my progress and offering support. Above all, I am grateful to my husband, Ken Haase, who faithfully read drafts, listened to me, and helped me think through places where I was stuck, prayed with and for me, encouraged me along the way, patiently endured piles of books and papers in our living space, and loved me through the whole process.

THE LEADER'S SOUL

TWENTY-FIRST-CENTURY LEADERS are rewarded for their drive, decisiveness, productivity, and long work hours. In such an environment, what happens to the soul of the leader? Too often, it shrivels and dies, resulting in harm to the leader and to the organization the leader serves.

The past decade has witnessed scandal after scandal: in business, in nonprofits, in religious institutions. Leaders give in to pressures to cook the books, to cut quality to make a quick buck, or to the allure of greed, lust, and power. Businesses lose their reputations and their customers. Public institutions lose the confidence of their constituencies. Churches lose the trust of their members. This world of scandals desperately needs leaders with soul.

Even short of scandal, leaders can easily drift toward burnout. The dream that originally drew leaders to their work loses its luster. Leaders find themselves going through the motions, ground down by the daily pressures of increasing the next quarter's profits, responding to the daily complaints of employees and constituents, and succumbing to the seeming inevitability of mediocrity.

This burnout spreads from the top down. Employees, after all, long to work in institutions that exhibit integrity. When they sense a lack of congruence with a company's purpose, employees disengage. Studies on employee engagement show that in the typical company worldwide, only 21 percent of the employees are fully engaged, 41 percent do enough to get by, and 38 percent are partially or completely disengaged.[1] Disengaged employees lack motivation and lack commitment to their company's mission, resulting in a dip in productivity, organizational effectiveness, and profitability. Companies with integrity, companies who live the values they espouse and treat their employees and customers with respect and fairness, attract better employees, keep those employees engaged, and earn higher profits.[2] While studies on engagement have primarily focused on for-profit companies, the findings are also relevant to the nonprofit sector. Nonprofits with high employee engagement can also expect to exhibit high morale, low turnover, and strong organizational effectiveness.

When facing such challenges as burnout and erosion of integrity, where can leaders find the help they need to keep their souls as alert as their minds and bodies? Business schools aren't designed to teach soul formation. The typical company environment doesn't help form the soul. On the contrary, the typical business school education de-forms the soul[3] as does the typical organizational environment. The best courses and books on leadership often mention the need for soul, but business schools and corporations exist in an environment that doesn't allow the theme of soul to take center stage. While a growing number of pioneering courses on leading with soul have been added to the curriculum as electives at a number of business schools, too often the seeds these courses plant don't have the opportunity to grow to maturity. Because such courses are usually countercultural in the business school environment, their influence wanes once students complete the course and move on to other courses that either don't nurture the growth of the seeds planted or even, by contradicting the principles taught in the soul-based courses, uproot the seedlings altogether.

There is more to leadership with soul than might be imagined, and teaching it requires examples and a different kind of language than the social-scientific language that dominates the business school environment. Courses on leading with soul have yet to be mainstreamed, to be integrated into the business school curriculum.[4] Too often, the message leaders absorb is that they must sell their souls in order to be effective leaders. Nonprofits and religious institutions, in an effort to promote efficiency and effectiveness (both laudable goals in themselves), mimic the soul-killing practices of corporations. As Ian Mitroff and Elizabeth Denton point out in *A Spiritual Audit of Corporate America,* "Today's organizations are impoverished spiritually, and many of their most important problems are due to this impoverishment."[5] Soul formation for leaders doesn't exist in the places business and organizational leaders receive their preparation.

Myriad forces have converged to create this state of affairs. The primary force, the rise of modern science over the past 350 years, has caused Western culture (which increasingly influences leadership in other parts of the world as well) to focus on the external to the detriment of the internal. While modern science has made many positive contributions to Western culture, contributions that all but the most Luddite of twenty-first-century Westerners would extol, our single focus has made us myopic. Alan Wallace summarizes the situation succinctly:

> While science has enthralled first Euro-American society and now most of the world with its progress in illuminating the nature of the external, physical world, I shall argue that it has eclipsed earlier knowledge of the nature of the inner reality of consciousness. In this regard, we in the modern West are unknowingly living in a dark age.[6]

This eclipsed knowledge of the inner reality of consciousness has distorted Western understandings of leadership, causing leaders and leadership scholars to focus on external results to the exclusion of internal growth and development. In everything they learn about leadership, whether in their training or in the reinforcement they receive on the job, leaders are taught to focus on external results. They are taught that outward results matter, while the inner life does not. What is measured becomes what is real. Because external results are measured and the inner life is ignored, the soul fades into oblivion.

Of course, there is nothing wrong with focusing on external results. Certainly, leaders must focus on the results of their leadership in order to face reality directly. Assessing results and adjusting one's leadership according to the consequences of one's actions is one of the fruits of good leadership.

At the same time, when roots don't receive the nourishment they need, the fruit and even the branches eventually wither. Long after its inner strength has begun to erode, a tree may look outwardly strong, especially to the untrained eye. It's only when a strong wind knocks down the once-mighty tree that it becomes clear to the untrained onlooker that its roots died long ago. The external results lauded by those who study leadership depend upon the internal. Yet, paradoxically, the internal is largely a taboo subject in mainstream leadership and management literature. Like arborists trying to improve the health of a tree while ignoring the roots, leadership scholars, by and large, have been blind to a significant dimension of leadership. In *The Soul of a Leader,* we'll pay attention to those roots and how to nourish and care for them.

Furthermore, as if this cultural focus on the external to the exclusion of the internal weren't enough to thoroughly erode a leader's soul, leaders who want to lead with soul find themselves up against a second influential force in Western culture: individualism, which results in a Lone Ranger mentality of leadership. This mentality, so firmly embraced by Western culture, sits squarely against the wisdom of spiritual traditions. Spiritual teachers know that souls need one another in order to flourish. Leaders who long to lead with soul find themselves in inner conflict when they bump into the cultural expectation that they should solve all their problems on their own — that they shouldn't need to draw on others' support. At one level, they know that they desperately need to share their problems with those with whom they can share their souls. On the other hand, they know that to admit this need will likely be interpreted by those whose opinions they value as a sign of weakness.

On occasion, leaders who have had the good fortune to receive soul formation and who happen to find themselves working in institutions hospitable to leading with soul are able to forge an alliance between the internal and external skills of leadership. But often such an alliance doesn't last long, for two reasons. First, such leaders often find themselves alone, isolated pioneers disconnected from leaders in other organizations who are attempting the same thing. Without peers traveling a similar path, most leaders can survive as heroic pioneers only for so long before they succumb to the pressures to conform to the culture. Second, such leaders often lack internal support for soulful leadership within the organizations they're leading. How often, for example, does a board ask its leader, "How is it with your soul?" Or how often will an institution reimburse a leader for a training program that promises to renew his soul?

Such lack of support for a leader's soul is short-sighted, since the people a leader leads suffer mightily when the leader's soul shrivels. As Parker Palmer puts it in his definition of a leader: "A leader is someone with the power to project either shadow or light onto some part of the world and onto the lives of the people who dwell there."[7]

The soul of a leader faces threats from every side. Therefore, those for whom the leader carries responsibility experience vulnerability.

Drawing on the work of Bernard Lonergan and Daniel Helminiak, I have argued elsewhere for the reintegration of the internal and the external in both the study and practice of leadership.[8] Both internal soul formation and external skills, I believe, are necessary for effective, inspired, ethical leadership over the long haul. The present book builds on the foundation of that earlier academic work and on a

decade and a half of study and practice, by explicating practical principles of soulful leadership. In this book, I draw on practical examples to
demonstrate how the inner and the outer complement one another.
Partners in the dance, the inner and the outer move together, hand
in hand.

In addition to pointing out the inner and outer aspects of leading
with soul, this book will demonstrate the process of transformation
that occurs within a leader who perseveres to the end, the parallel process of transformation that occurs within that leader's organization,
and the place of spiritual guidance in the process.

In this book I address the following questions:

1. What would it look like, both for the leader and for the organi-
    zation a leader serves, for a leader to cultivate the inner life, to
    step off the treadmill, to nurture the soul?

2. Where can a leader turn for formation of the soul?

3. How can leaders find the resources they need for ongoing nour-
    ishment for the soul in the midst of the pressures of leadership?

4. Can a leader realistically expect to maintain a healthy soul over
    the long haul? What is the process of spiritual transformation
    that occurs when a leader perseveres to the end, and how can
    that process be supported?

This book, in addressing these questions, offers soul formation
and maintenance for leaders. It outlines principles that any leader can
follow, with examples showing how leaders put these principles into
practice. This book is about how a leader becomes an ethical leader
who leads with integrity, and about how such a leader stays on the
path of soul when inner and outer forces challenge that commitment.
It shows that leading with soul *is* possible over the long haul, and it
demonstrates the remarkable organizational outcomes that can result
from soulful leadership.

My definition of "soul" is broad. Spiritual writers use "soul" to speak not about something a person has but about who a person most deeply is.[9] In my understanding of soul, this deep essence of a person may find expression through religious faith or it may find expression in other ways. Soul is the way that emotional or relational depth is honored and the way that yearnings for development or evolution are given space, whether in a religious context or in other contexts.[10]

This book is based on interviews. In most cases, I interviewed multiple people from each organization represented in order to get multiple perspectives on the leader highlighted. I also read all the published material I could find on the leader and the organization — both material published by the organization itself (in print or on the Web) as well as material published about the leader and the organization by others. In the only case in which I did not do any interviews, I was in the process of arranging an interview with Anita Roddick when she died suddenly. I decided to include her and her work at the Body Shop in the book despite the lack of an interview, because of the important impact she made by leading with soul, and because of the wealth of published material that exists about her and about the Body Shop.

Part 1, "Choosing the Path," focuses on how leaders can take the first steps toward leading with soul. The three chapters in part 1, "Following the Heart," "Finding Partners," and "Daring to Dream," all outline principles of soul formation for leaders. Illustrated with examples from the lives of leaders in business, health care, entertainment, and nonprofits, Part 1 shows leaders taking the first halting steps of soulful leadership and then learning to walk the path.

Part 2, "Staying on Track," examines how leaders can stay the course in the midst of the challenges that inevitably arise once the newness of soul-based leadership has worn off. "Keeping Mission at the Fore," "Practicing Gratitude," and "Battling for the Soul," the three chapters of part 2, all outline principles of staying focused, again illustrated with examples from the lives of real leaders in real organizations who face pressures that could push them off the path.

Part 3, "Persevering to the End," considers principles that help leaders persevere over the long haul. "Breaking the Cycle of Violence" examines the shift that occurs in leaders and the situations they encounter when nonviolence is practiced. "Persevering to the End" considers the process of transformation that occurs in leaders and organizations who practice the principles in the book. The final chapter, "Finding Spiritual Guidance," demonstrates the need for and the value of spiritual guidance in a leader's life.

Each chapter ends with a few queries. Rooted in the Quaker tradition, queries are open-ended questions designed to encourage reflection. With no right or wrong answers, the queries invite the reader to reflect, both personally and organizationally, on the themes of the chapter.

A final note: In this book, I define leadership broadly. Everyone is a leader in his or her sphere of influence. While the CEO of a company is clearly a leader, so are managers and supervisors in their own spheres of influence. So are housekeepers or nursing assistants when they lead informally with co-workers or patients. The examples in the book are primarily from organizational leadership, but some of the leadership work illustrated, such as that of Desmond Tutu, The Edge of the rock band U2, and Clarena Tolson, streets commissioner for the city of Philadelphia, goes beyond traditional organizational leadership. The principles apply anywhere. Parents are leaders. Teachers are leaders. Committee chairs are leaders. Anyone can apply these principles and lead with soul in any sphere, large or small. As you read this book and reflect on the queries, don't sell yourself short — remember the many places in your life where you influence others. As you see the ripple effect of the actions of the leaders in this book, remember that your actions, too, set off a ripple effect.

Happy leading!

PART ONE

CHOOSING THE PATH

Chapter One

FOLLOWING
THE HEART

I N 1968, Tom Chappell was enjoying a successful career in insurance in the greater Philadelphia area. Nevertheless, he and his wife, Kate, felt that something was missing. They longed for a rural setting in which to raise their children, and they wanted work that contributed to their passion for natural products and a clean environment. So in the spring of the next year, they uprooted their young family and drove to Maine, with only a dream and a prayer, to find a new life.

Tom and Kate's experience is not atypical for the leader taking the first halting steps on the path toward leading with soul. Following the heart typically involves three stages: paying attention, taking the first step, and stumbling. This chapter will outline these three stages, illustrating each one with examples of leaders who experienced them. In addition to Tom and Kate Chappell, co-founders of the personal-care product manufacturer Tom's of Maine, the illustrations will include Meg Clapp, who became director of the 250-person pharmacy department at Massachusetts General Hospital in Boston, and Ken Melrose, who became CEO of Toro, a leading manufacturer of lawnmowers and other landscaping products.

Paying Attention

The heart makes its desires known in many ways. Yet in the hustle and bustle of the daily demands of leadership, it's easy for leaders to ignore what their hearts are trying to tell them. The focus in Western culture on external reality to the exclusion of the internal eclipses the stirrings of the heart. Yet the leader who makes space in the midst of the busyness and musters the courage to pay attention to the stirrings of the heart will reap rich rewards.

For Tom and Kate Chappell, paying attention to the heart meant listening to the stirrings of discontent. Though Tom's career was advancing well, they knew they needed more. Their hearts told them that they had a different contribution to make to the world. As they listened to the desires of their hearts, they began to see what that contribution might be. Kate reflects:

> Both Tom and I have a strong sense of paying attention to what is calling us. That has been true, not just for the business, but for other aspects of our life where we've been at a crossroad. We try to be reflective and prayerful about what the next step is. If you allow it, the spiritual becomes an important voice that you listen to. I think that in our culture, though, we tend to dismiss that voice, we tend to ignore it, push it down, and go on with business as usual.

Paying attention requires courage. For Tom and Kate, it would have been easy to stay comfortable, secure in Tom's steady job with a good income. It would have been easy to pay attention briefly, and then dismiss the voice of the heart as too idealistic or as something to listen to a few years down the road. But Tom and Kate had the courage to keep paying attention, even though they didn't know where their hearts would lead them.

LIKE TOM AND KATE, Meg Clapp, a resident in pharmacy at Massachusetts General Hospital, paid attention when her heart told her that the path she was heading down was not the path for her. She paid attention when her heart said that the traditional practices of leadership in her organization weren't working for her. Beginning in her residency, Meg found herself fascinated with leadership, observing each of her supervisors and the impact each one's leadership style had on the department. Quickly moving up the ranks into health care leadership, Meg observed a notable disconnect between the supposedly effective traditional command-and-control leadership style of the senior people at the hospital and its demoralizing effect on her and on her subordinates. Her heart told her there must be a better way. Paying attention to her heart rather than to her mentors required courage, especially when her mentors offered well-articulated arguments for their methods, while she had no clear alternative to propose.

KEN MELROSE PAID ATTENTION to his heart in 1973 when he was transferred from his job as marketing director at the Toro Company's Minneapolis headquarters to head up the newly acquired playground equipment company Game Time in southwestern Michigan. He paid attention when his heart told him he couldn't lead in the way the previous leader had led. While the former Game Time president had founded the company and worked there for years, Ken was a neophyte in the business. He knew about marketing lawnmowers, not running a playground equipment company. But Game Time's employees expected the president to make most of the substantive decisions. While Ken might have been tempted to try to learn everything about the business quickly and assume the role of decision maker for the substantive decisions, his heart told him the company needed something different. Not only would he be overreaching his competency, but the employees would not be well served by a leader who assumed too much responsibility for calling the shots.[1] Ken paid attention as his heart led him down a new path.

Although they didn't know where it would lead them, Tom and Kate, Meg, and Ken knew they could pay attention and trust the heart to speak.

Taking the First Step

Taking the first step is never easy. Naysayers, inside and out, will insist that safety lies in staying where you are. Why step onto an uncharted course? What possible good can result from venturing into the unknown? In this dark age of contemporary Western culture in which inner reality has been eclipsed, naysayers don't understand the need for stepping out in response to the heart. They fear what will happen to anyone who takes the first step of following the heart. Even more, they fear for those leaders who step out in response to the heart and for those the leaders lead.

In everything they have learned about leadership, leaders have learned to focus on the external. The outward results matter, they have learned, while the inner life does not. Because the inner life is ignored, the heart fades into oblivion. Stepping out in response to the heart flies in the face of everything that leaders have learned.

But the heart knows that the way will be revealed and that it will be good. The heart serves as a compass, helping the leader take the first step, then another, then another.

MEG CLAPP TOOK THE FIRST STEP when she pioneered new approaches to leadership for the MGH pharmacy department. Unlike Tom Chappell, Meg stayed in her profession. But with her new style of leadership, she struck out on her own. For Meg, the first step meant saying no to the methods she saw modeled by her superiors. The first step meant breaking with the command-and-control culture, a culture that gave all the power to those on top and discounted those at the lower levels. Meg sought another way, and although she was unsure of the path she was taking, she took the step of trying something new with her charges. She began by honoring each employee and treating each one with dignity and respect. She told them she valued their input. She included them in planning and decision making.

Accustomed to being told what to do, the employees at Game Time came to Ken Melrose with major decisions. When the purchasing manager came to Ken to ask how much steel to order, Ken took the first step and told him that he didn't know. Shocked, the purchasing manager pleaded for direction, claiming that the previous president always told him how much to order. Ken could have given in to the pressure to conform to the company culture. He could have learned what he needed to know, then told the purchasing manager how much steel to order. But he didn't. Instead, he saw the moment as an opportunity—an opportunity to take the first step away from a dependent workforce and toward an empowered workforce. He explained to the purchasing manager, "I don't know how much steel to order. I've never done this before. But I do know some of the things I'd need to know to make the decision, such as how many merry-go-rounds the production manager was planning to make. Together, we can answer the question." Corralling the inventory manager, the production manager, and the sales manager to find out how much inventory was in the barn, how much steel was required to make a merry-go-round, and what the sales forecast was, Ken asked many questions. By reflecting upon the answers with the purchasing manager, Ken helped him make his own decision. Ken had taken the first step.

Tom Chappell took the first step when he left his lucrative insurance job in Philadelphia and headed toward the unknown. He and Kate left their home, uprooted their family, and headed north, with only the heart to lead. In Kate's words:

One is on a journey, and at various phases in a life you find that what was working before is no longer working and there is a reason, and that is the point at which God is calling you to turn in some way, to face life in a different way so you can see your new path. It's harder sometimes to break out of that and go in a new direction and do something that people aren't expecting you to do. I think at those points, if you can get in touch with what you feel is your center — for me, that is God is within me — then I feel I'm not alone in taking the first step on a new path.

They moved to southern Maine so that Tom could work with his father, an entrepreneur. While they didn't know if this would be a long-term commitment, they knew they needed to take the first step so that subsequent steps could reveal themselves.

Stumbling

Like toddlers learning to walk, leaders who take the first step in response to the heart inevitably stumble. In a world that expects leaders to be successful, stumbling requires courage. With Western culture's focus on results, on the next quarter's profits, leaders who stumble don't receive much grace.

While focusing on success is important, so is grace. When leaders don't have room to stumble, their hearts lose their passion. Stumbling will always be part of following the heart, and leaders need permission to stumble, permission from themselves and from those to whom they are accountable, if they are to do their best work.

KEN MELROSE STUMBLED at Game Time as he made mistakes and learned along with his employees. He would sometimes ask the wrong questions or not be able to recognize errors in the answers he received, for example, the time the sales forecast he was given was wrong, resulting in the company's manufacturing too many merry-go-rounds. He modeled what he was teaching: that mistakes are necessary for learning, and that, as long as learning occurs, mistakes (up to a point) are to be applauded, not punished.

When Ken returned to Toro's corporate offices in 1976 to head up the outdoor power equipment division, he stumbled again as he sought to mainstream what he had learned in his three years at Game Time into the Toro corporate culture. He started an informal Friday morning managers' group with a focus on how to put people first in the workplace, starting with valuing people in the decision-making process, and learned how hard it is to make a dent in corporate culture if the leadership at the top doesn't support the change. At the same time, as he persevered and reflected back later, he found that he had sown the seeds for the changes in the corporate culture that came five to ten years later:

> The natural conclusion for me was that unless you're at the top, you can't change the culture. That was my first conclusion. But I found that in the organization, there were several managers and a few officers (director level and vice-president) that really wanted to manage and lead differently, to talk through how we made decisions, to be mindful of what the impact on people was and how we involved people in these processes. That was a sustaining thing that gave us a lift when we left the meeting that day and thought about it over the weekend. We came back on Monday charged up to infuse more people-orientation into what we did, more caring and compassion. It really was very helpful because a lot of those people were still around when we were forming the new Toro in the early 1980s, and they remarked, "That was one of the grassroots things that helped form our culture. We were forming the culture of the eighties without even knowing we were doing it."

And in 1981, when Ken became CEO of Toro, inheriting a sick company, he stumbled yet again. Ultimately forced to lay off over half the workforce, Ken and his team had to make some tough decisions, and he stumbled as he sought humane ways of laying employees off and restructuring the company. It was at this time that he began to draw more deeply on his faith:

> Every day I was spending time with people coming to my office crying, "Why do I have to leave? Why are you terminating me? We've been friends for five or ten years. I always thought you were one of the good guys, but now I have to leave." I started thinking, "What did I do to deserve this? This is not me. I hate doing this."
>
> I thought, "I can't do this by myself. I need God's help here." So I put up a sign: "God meant you to be here now." I put it up on the wall right above my telephone, so I could look up and see it whenever I was on the phone. I didn't tell many people this but I was really scared and I was awed by the responsibility. I needed a reminder that this was God's will and he meant for me to be here and he meant for it to be now. And there's a reason for that and just hang in there because you're not alone. That's when I really began to draw on my faith.

While Ken Melrose and his team ultimately built Toro into a very successful company again,[2] in his early days as CEO it was not yet clear what the outcome of his leadership would be. Ken stumbled as he sought to follow his heart.

MEG CLAPP STUMBLED as she sought to find a new way of leading. Lacking formal training in leadership, she educated herself, reading every management book she could get her hands on. She worked with her staff and used them as guinea pigs to try out every new theory she discovered to see if it worked for them. One of her mistakes, she admits in hindsight, was the "Valentine's Day Massacre," as it became known among her employees. It occurred the day she reorganized the department on a dime, and staff members found themselves wandering aimlessly, unsure of their assigned tasks or teammates.

Yet Meg found that she learned from her mistakes. And her employees forgave her, because they knew she would make whatever changes were needed to make it work, they knew she was not wedded to her ideas, and they knew she had their best interests at heart. As Meg says, "I tell my staff, 'I am here to bring out the best in you so that our patients win.'" Her staff believed her because she walked her talk.

For Meg, stumbling and falling was a necessary part of learning to walk, learning to lead with soul. Eventually her failures led to success. For example, the Valentine's Day Massacre reorganization broke the stranglehold of the department's hierarchical leadership model. Though the reorganization in itself was very rocky in the beginning, it opened the way for a matrix model of leadership where leadership in the pharmacy department was organized around individual gifts rather than around predetermined roles.

Tom and Kate Chappell stumbled as they sought to find their way. With only their entrepreneurial spirit to guide them, they first moved to southern Maine, where Tom worked for his father's company. After two years, Tom realized that working with his father was not his path, and he and Kate left to start their own company.

Tom and Kate stumbled early in their own business as they experimented with developing natural products. They learned that stumbling is part of the process, that innovation is all about taking a few steps, stumbling, and getting up again. A friend offered them a $5,000 loan, and they threw themselves headlong into developing the product of their dreams. Although their first product, a nonpolluting detergent for cleaning dairies, wasn't a moneymaker, it led to their second product, a nonpolluting laundry detergent dubbed Clearlake, which was packaged in returnable plastic bottles. A modest financial success, Clearlake laundry detergent kept them afloat as they experimented with soaps, shampoos, and then toothpaste. In their early years, they stumbled and learned and grew, with some products that were total flops and others that were mild successes.[3]

THROUGH THEIR STUMBLING, Ken Melrose, Meg Clapp, and Tom and Kate Chappell learned that their hearts would serve as their compass. True north, the way of the heart, would reveal itself as they stumbled, fell, and began the process anew, each time learning a little more about how to lead with soul.

Conclusion

Following the heart is like learning to walk. Paying attention, taking the first step, and stumbling all prepare the toddler for walking. Likewise, paying attention, taking the first step, and stumbling all prepare the leader for following the heart. In a leadership world in which leaders who follow their hearts face threats from every side, following the heart requires courage. In the rough-and-tumble culture of leadership where the inner life is ignored, where what is measured becomes real, the heart fades into oblivion. Leaders who follow their hearts assert a different reality.

Leaders who follow their hearts take halting steps, make false starts, and fall frequently. Stumbling is part of the process; it teaches the leader what the path will be like and how to accept the bumps along the way.

Questions

1. What practices help you pay attention to your heart? How are you paying attention to your heart now?

2. In what ways has the environment around you threatened your heart with oblivion? How have you asserted a different reality?

3. What first step is your heart beckoning you to take?

4. How have you learned from your stumbling? How are you currently taking risks and learning from your stumblings?

Chapter Two

FINDING PARTNERS

A RRIVING AT ST. JOHN MEDICAL CENTER in Longview, Washington, as CEO in early 2002, Medrice Coluccio encountered a desperate situation. Morale had plummeted, patient satisfaction was low, and finances were in ruins. To make matters worse, the Longview area, already one of the poorest communities in Washington State, had been dealt additional blows by the post-9/11 recession. Medrice had followed her heart to St. John Medical Center. Now what?

Medrice knew that she couldn't possibly turn the desperate situation around alone. How was she to proceed?

Following the heart gets a leader started on the path of leading with soul. Stumbling and falling and learning to walk, a leader haltingly follows the heart. What happens next? Those who follow the heart soon find that they need partners. Like following the heart, finding partners is a process involving ups and downs. This chapter will consider three principles of finding partners: speaking the heart's truth, seeking resonance, and inviting partnership. Each principle will be illustrated with examples of leaders who lived it: Medrice Coluccio, Tom Henry, General Manager of Landry's Bicycles in Boston, and

Rabbi Samuel Karff, cofounder of the Texas health-care-based Sacred Vocation program.

Speaking the Heart's Truth

To find partners, a leader must begin by speaking the heart's truth. Taking the first halting steps of following the heart requires courage, as noted in chapter 1, and speaking the heart's truth to the world at large requires even more courage. Furthermore, speaking the heart's truth in the search for partners requires admitting that one needs help. If there is anything that Western culture tells leaders even more loudly than "Focus on external results," it is "Do it alone." To admit that one needs help is often seen as a sign of weakness. Yet, as noted earlier, this Lone Ranger mentality of leadership sits squarely against a fundamental principle of leading with soul, articulated by spiritual teachers of all traditions: souls need one another in order to flourish. Speaking the heart's truth in the search for partners requires a deep trust that those one leads will be better served when one finds partners. Speaking the heart's truth requires the courage to stand against the conventional wisdom of the West.

MEDRICE COLUCCIO SPOKE HER HEART'S TRUTH from the very beginning of the interview process. For Medrice, following her heart meant seeking a position where her soul could flourish and where she could help others' souls flourish. During the interview process, Medrice spoke about the kind of institution she sought to serve — an institution that put mission first. She spoke about how she had been drawn to St. John Medical Center by the Sisters of St. Joseph of Peace, the founding religious community of Peace Health (St. John's parent body). She put her desire to lead from her soul, to lead from the institution's mission, before the board of trustees, before the corporate executive officers, before her potential employees. For Medrice, speaking the heart's truth required courage. The hospital itself was in trouble; as Medrice herself admitted, "The hospital was not well. We were on the respirator big time." To go against conventional business wisdom at such a time, to focus on mission first, believing that putting mission first would eventually result in increased patient satisfaction and a better bottom line, required courage. Medrice knew that some would disagree with her. She knew that some would label her unrealistic. Yet she continued to speak her heart's truth, convinced that doing so would lead her to the partners she needed.

T OM HENRY, NOW GENERAL MANAGER of Landry's Bicycles in Boston, spoke his heart's truth in 1987 when he became a co-owner of the family bicycle dealership owned by his brother and sister-in-law. A visionary by nature, Tom believed that Landry's could become the best bicycle shop in the country. He believed that independent bicycle shops could band together to lobby for better conditions for cyclists, and that they could regain and even increase the market share they had lost to the "big box" stores like Wal-Mart. He believed in bicycling for a better world. Tom spoke his heart's truth when he put his vision before his brother and sister-in-law, Peter and Jeanne Henry, before employees, before other bike shop owners, and before other cyclists.

Tom took risks. In a world of fierce competition among independent bike shops, he shared his vision of cooperation. In a small-business culture focused on survival, he shared his vision of becoming the best. In the tough world of Massachusetts politics, he lobbied for his vision of bike paths everywhere. Tom consistently spoke his heart's truth within Landry's, in the larger bicycle retail community, and in public-policy settings.

S AMUEL KARFF, A RETIRED RABBI, spoke his heart's truth after a hospital stay in Houston, Texas. His experience as a dependent and vulnerable hospital patient caused Rabbi Karff to notice how equally dependent and vulnerable his caregivers were. From his patient bed, Rabbi Karff observed that the hospital could be just as demoralizing for employees as it was for those they cared for. He wondered how the sense of calling, the sense of sacred vocation that had originally brought health care workers to the field, could be rekindled. How could a sense of dignity and independence be restored to health care workers and patients alike?

Rabbi Karff spoke his heart's truth when he shared his vision of reclaiming health care providers' sense of sacred vocation. He spoke his heart's truth when he spoke to hospital administrators, physicians, and researchers about his vision. He spoke his heart's truth when he spoke to potential funders. Speaking his heart's truth required courage as Rabbi Karff encountered naysayers: those who believed his vision was too religious for a secular hospital, those who believed his vision was too idealistic in the fast-paced world of contemporary health care, and those who believed his vision would be impossible to fund. Against all odds, Rabbi Karff persisted in speaking his heart's truth.

Seeking Resonance

Leaders who speak their hearts' truth in the search for partners then seek resonance. They look for the eyes that light up when they share vision, the ears that perk up when they tell stories of hope. They are on the alert for the hearts, once hurt by the betrayal of hope they put in former leaders, that are ready to take the first cautious steps of hoping again.

As Rabbi Karff spoke his heart's truth widely, he sought resonance. He watched for those whose eyes lit up when he spoke about re-kindling health care providers' sense of sacred vocation. He noticed those who seemed energized by the idea of starting with frontline workers. He noted those who grasped the relationships between en-ergized health care providers, satisfied patients, and a transformed workplace. He watched and waited, seeking fertile ground for his vision.

As Tom Henry spoke his heart's truth with his colleagues at Landry's, he kept his eyes open for those who resonated with his vision to be the best bike shop in the United States. When he shared his vision for a coalition of independent bike shops with colleagues outside Landry's, he had ears to hear where the enthusiasm lay for what could be achieved by lobbying together and by joining together to increase market share. When he shared his vision with Boston area cyclists, he had eyes to see the passion others had for joining him to expand MassBike, the cyclist organization intent on improving bicycling conditions in Massachusetts.

As she spoke her heart's truth in the interview process, Medrice Coluccio sought resonance. She noticed those whose faces beamed when she talked about mission, those whose ears perked up when she talked about engagement. Medrice had eyes to see where the fertile ground was for the work she longed to do. Through thick and thin, during the interview process and after accepting the position, Medrice kept seeking resonance with her heart's yearnings. After nearly two hundred interviews, convinced that many at St. John Medical Center and the larger Peace Health system desired the same things she desired, she accepted the position.

Inviting Partnership

After leaders speak their heart's truth and once they seek resonance, they are ready to invite partnership. Those who lead with soul seek others who understand that souls need one another in order to flourish. They seek others who will take a stand against the Lone Ranger mentality of leadership. They know that other leaders who want to lead with soul find themselves in inner conflict when they bump into the cultural expectation that they should solve all their problems on their own, that they shouldn't need to draw on others' support. At one level, they know they desperately need to be with those with whom they can share their souls. On the other hand, they know that to admit this need will likely be interpreted by those whose opinions they value as a sign of weakness. Those committed to leading with soul invite partnership, invite other leaders to take the risk of admitting they need help.

ONCE MEDRICE COLUCCIO MOVED into the role of CEO, she began to invite people to partner with her. She knew that the turnaround of the unhealthy hospital would require a strong team. Early on, Medrice demonstrated her commitment to partnership by moving her office from the "White House," a separate administrative building so nicknamed by employees, to the main hospital building, so that she could be in the midst of St. John's workforce and continue to listen to their day-to-day struggles. Medrice soon discovered that she had to prove herself. With morale low, trust didn't come easily. Employees needed to see for themselves that Medrice's desire for partnership was authentic. With her original training and experience as a nurse, Medrice knew her employees' challenges firsthand. Every day, she spent time out on the floor with frontline caregivers, and gradually Medrice won the employees' respect and trust.

Medrice began a mission-based strategic planning process, inviting as many people as possible to partner with her. She started simply, with focus groups, asking three questions:

1. What is working?

2. What isn't working? and

3. If you could wave your magic wand, what would you like to see different come out of our health care ministry here?

Within a few months of assuming the role of CEO, Medrice had assembled a design team for the strategic plan — strong partners who would work with her to determine the direction of the hospital. Using the information gathered from the focus groups, the design team began to construct a mission-based strategic plan, from the bottom up. The design team represented the full range of hospital employees, physicians, and board members. Everyone had a voice.

The team began by asking, "Can we be more than we are?" Answering in the affirmative, they asked further, "What would be marks of a successful strategic plan?" They identified ten, including:

- Deliver a believable and doable plan.

- Meet the medical and surgical needs of the community.

- Create pride in the workplace.

- Serve as a benchmark for health care in the region.

- Be economically viable.

With the success criteria in place to guide them, the team articulated a four-step planning process.

First, they *described the desired future state of St. John Medical Center.* They realized that the mission and vision statements needed to be clearly defined in order to articulate where they wanted to go, so they put their parent organization's mission statement front and center in their planning:

PEACE HEALTH MISSION STATEMENT

We carry on the healing ministry of Jesus Christ by promoting personal and community health, relieving pain and suffering, and treating each person in a loving and caring way.

They then articulated a vision statement for their particular region:

REGIONAL VISION STATEMENT

We are a health care ministry serving the Lower Columbia Region, recognized for excellence, strengthened by technical expertise, tempered by compassion, and delivered by dedicated people who share a heritage based on the belief that all life is precious.

Together, these two statements provided the plumb line the team needed to envision their desired future state.

Second, the design team recognized the *need to describe the current state of the institution,* in order to assess how far they needed to go to reach their desired future state. They took stock of their current commitments, identified the organizational and market barriers they faced, and examined internal and external limitations.

Third, the team *evaluated their capability to move from where they were to where they wanted to be.* To do this, the design team translated the mission and vision statements into concrete goals in such areas of the hospital's work as patient care, leadership development, improvement of facilities, and employee pride and loyalty. With concrete goals articulated, the team assessed their resources and capability of achieving the goals.

Fourth, the team *developed an incremental master plan.* They examined activities that were already in place and initiated new activities that would meet the goals, sequencing them over a five-year period, with the activities organized into ten strategic initiatives.

By the time the board adopted the strategic plan in the fall of 2002, strong partnerships had already been built, and there was widespread enthusiasm for the new direction.

Then the real work began. If the turnaround was going to happen in five years, people had to be engaged. Medrice invited a different partner to "champion" each of the nine strategic initiatives, tapping a staff nurse, a physician, and a sister from the hospital's founding religious community, in addition to more traditional leaders. By carefully inviting unconventional "champions" as partners, Coluccio made certain that each initiative would get the time, energy, and enthusiasm it deserved. Furthermore, in recognition that "championing" takes significant work, Coluccio reduced each champion's workload to make space for the strategic initiative work.

By inviting partnerships, Medrice had succeeded in creating a mission-based strategic plan and a strong implementation team. The sick hospital was on the road to recovery.

ONCE TOM HENRY HAD IDENTIFIED PEOPLE inside and outside of Landry's Bicycles who resonated with his vision, he invited partnerships. First, he invited partners within the company to help Landry's be all that it could be internally and to help Landry's accomplish its mission.

For the co-owners, for example, working at a family business like Landry's involved all the blessings and curses that come with working with one's own family. While working together went smoothly 90 percent of the time, the executive team was plagued the other 10 percent of the time by repeated patterns of stepping on one another's toes. In order to become better partners, the executive team committed to working together to overcome their 10 percent gap. They realized that they needed to model what a team could be at its best if they expected the best from other teams in the seventy-five-employee company. By partnering with another (nonfamily) member, adding him to the executive team, and doing extensive self-awareness work, the executive team learned to value each other's gifts, see the shadow side of their own gifts, and practice confession and humility. For instance, when Tom arrived ten minutes late to an important all-company meeting, the new nonfamily member of the executive team called him on it. Tom apologized to the gathered meeting and committed to changing his pattern.

Closing the 10 percent gap took a full year of hard work, but by the end of the year, the executive team realized that all the work had been worth the effort. Rather than stepping on one another's toes and building up resentments that sapped energy and commitment, the team had learned to notice toes sooner and thus step on them less frequently! More importantly, when someone did step on someone's toes, confession and forgiveness followed quickly. By inviting a partner from outside, the family business owners learned how to be better partners to one another.

Because of the success they had experienced on the executive team, Tom invited another partner, this time a human resources expert he had met through Seeing Things Whole (see below, p. 45), to help with values-based leadership training for all employees. He wanted Landry's teams to learn the same kinds of skills the executive team had learned.

In a practice unusual for a seasonal retail business, Landry's commits to year-round employment and training for its employees. During the low-revenue winter months, the company invests in its employees through leadership training. Seventy percent of the training consists of hands-on activities: role playing, real-time interactions with other employees, and exercises designed to enable self-awareness. While assertiveness and vision contribute to a salesperson's success, the shadow side of those traits is often an inability to listen to others and an insensitivity to the needs of the customer (or fellow employee). The human resources partner's leadership training included helping employees see their own and others' gifts and helping them identify the shadow side of those gifts. By recognizing the constellation of gifts on a team, employees came to value one another as essential to the whole, building stronger partnerships. They also came to see the need for humility and confession whenever they tripped over the shadow side of their gifts and stepped on one another's toes.

Second, in addition to inviting outside partners to help build effective partnerships within the company, Tom encouraged partnerships outside the company. He called upon partners to help expand the Massachusetts Bicycle Coalition (MassBike), dedicated to serving the interests of the Massachusetts bicycling public through education and advocacy. He himself served as president of MassBike for three years, working together with others in the organization to improve cycling in the state. By joining forces with other cyclists and cycling groups, Tom and MassBike have achieved such goals as expanding the hours during which bikes are allowed on the subway and creating safe school bicycle routes for students.

Tom also invited partners to help strengthen the National Bike Summit, held annually in Washington, D.C. Founded in 2001, the National Bike Summit lobbies legislators regarding cycling issues. At the Bike Summit, sponsored by the League of American Bicyclists, cyclists and industry representatives can attend presentations dealing with legislation affecting cycling. They can also take the opportunity to lobby legislators and to recognize government officials who have helped improve conditions for cycling in America. For example, in 2005, Sen. John Kerry, in accepting the National Bicycle Advocacy award, spoke about how honored he felt to receive it, having been a bicycle enthusiast since childhood.

Tom also formed partnerships with others committed to the integration of values and business by becoming a founding member of "Seeing Things Whole." Both a model and a process created by Dick Broholm and David Specht, Seeing Things Whole links faith and organizational life. Springing from Christian roots, Seeing Things Whole also seeks to include wisdom from all religious traditions. Seeing Things Whole sponsors regular roundtables made up of representatives of four or five organizations that meet in the Boston area several times a year. At each roundtable meeting, one member organization presents a current challenge it is facing, and the group, guided by a trained facilitator, uses the Seeing Things Whole model and process to help illuminate the challenge.[1] Tom has invited other roundtable participants to partner with Landry's as temporary trustees. He maintains that Seeing Things Whole has in effect served as Landry's board of trustees over the years, helping the company stay true to its values and mission.

Partnership has now become a way of life at Landry's. The company's core values, displayed prominently in its four retail bicycle shops and on its website, declare partnerships with employees, other cyclists, the Seeing Things Whole network, and the world:

Our core values, which guide everything we do at Landry's Bicycles, include

◆ Treating all our customers as honored guests

◆ Connecting with the larger realm of bicycling

◆ Making the world a better place through our work

◆ Celebrating the quality of our people

◆ Fostering teamwork, open communication, honesty, and trust

◆ Taking intelligent risks

◆ Continuously improving how we do things

In addition, Landry's is a founding member of Seeing Things Whole, a professional network seeking to understand the intersection of faith and organizational life.[2]

By inviting partnerships, Tom Henry has chosen the path of leading with soul, gaining strength and guidance for keeping Landry's Bicycles grounded in its values.

LIKE MEDRICE COLUCCIO AND TOM HENRY, Rabbi Samuel Karff is a genius of strategic partnership. Rabbi Karff invited Dr. Benjamin Amick, a researcher at the University of Texas School of Public

Health, to partner with him when he asked for his help in cofounding the Sacred Vocation program. Rabbi Karff knew that what was impossible alone was possible when working together. Each of the two men worked within a different network, and each brought different skills to the project. Ben Amick agreed to join the partnership, and together they invited other partners to join them. They asked the McGovern Center for Health, Humanities, and the Human Spirit at the University of Texas Medical School to take the program under its wing as a partner, stressing the mutual benefits of the affiliation. The McGovern Center agreed, and Rabbi Karff, named a McGovern Center Senior Fellow, now offers frequent public lectures about Sacred Vocation, sponsored by the Center.

Rabbi Karff invited others to partner with him when he asked the leadership of St. Luke's Episcopal Hospital in Houston to work with him in designing a Sacred Vocation pilot program for their frontline caregivers. When the leaders agreed, Rabbi Karff invited the frontline caregivers to partner with him and the hospital leaders in designing the pilot program.

A three-phase program, Sacred Vocation started with small groups of eight to twelve employees learning to recognize their work as sacred vocation. In five ninety-minute sessions, employees share stories of what brought them to health care, how their work is connected to their spirituality, and how they understand vocation. Rabbi Karff underscores the importance of affirming all forms of spirituality represented in the groups — both those forms connected to established religions and those with no particular religious connection. One of the exercises requires participants to write their own obituaries, helping them reflect on what they want to be remembered for. Participants in Sacred Vocation share stories of the barriers that have prevented them from being healers, as they role-play situations and brainstorm coping tips. At the end of the first phase of the program, the group writes a Sacred Vocation Oath, taken publicly in a program graduation ceremony. A recent group of patient care technicians, for example, developed the following oath:

I will:

* Strive for outcomes that benefit all

* Comfort anxious and frightened patients

* Be caring and tender in all that I do

* Honor every patient with dignity and respect

* Heal patients physically, emotionally, and spiritually

* Listen and give hope to patients and their families

* Speak in a comforting and reassuring way

Nobody can take away my power to heal.

The second phase of Sacred Vocation focuses on improving the workplace. Rabbi Karff's partner Benjamin Amick invited management to be a partner in the pilot program, responsive to frontline caregivers' needs — and management agreed. In five sixty-minute small-group sessions, employees consider the changes management could make that would create a better environment for living out their sacred vocation at work. Through a facilitated action research process, representatives from different departments formulated an action plan, which they presented to management. These recommendations, divided into "minimal cost," "moderate cost," and "costly" categories, were made with a clear delineation of how their success would be measured. In a recent Sacred Vocation program, for example, a group of certified nursing assistants made twenty-seven recommendations to management, twenty-four of which were implemented. As a result, morale soared among the CNAs, and patient satisfaction increased dramatically.

Phase three focuses on ongoing implementation. Tailoring the particulars to the organization's needs, Ben Amick partners with staff and management to help integrate the Sacred Vocation program into the organization's ongoing life.

When budget cuts forced the program at St. Luke's Episcopal Hospital to close after the pilot project was completed, Rabbi Karff, not to be dissuaded, invited Episcopal Charities to partner with him in funding the Sacred Vocation program. Episcopal Charities accepted and has now helped fund Sacred Vocation programs at two clinics for low-income patients in Houston.

Now in its sixth year, the Sacred Vocation partnership has articulated a mission statement, which reads:

The Sacred Vocation Partnership is a collaboration between St. Luke's Episcopal Health Charities and the University of Texas Health Science Center Houston. This collaboration seeks to create beneficial and enduring changes in health, human service, and other not-for-profit organizations by helping individuals experience meaning in and through their work, thereby enhancing the quality of care and service.

At the San Jose Clinic, a Houston clinic for low-income patients, two teams have completed the training. The first team, made up of patient care assistants serving on the front lines, found the training so helpful that they recommended it to administrators. The administrators, including the executive director, took their advice and found the training transformative. They discovered that the program strengthened relationships and "made a huge difference in our day-to-day operation," according to Stacie Cokinos, executive director of the clinic.

Rabbi Karff has also partnered with the medical school at the University of Texas Medical Center, where the topic of spirituality and healing is an integral part of medical students' training. At the medical school, faculty recognize that healing is determined not only by doctors' ability to apply medical technology, but also by the relationship between doctor and patient.

Most recently, Baylor University Medical Center at Dallas signed on as a Sacred Vocation partner. Participants included over 145 patient care technicians and assistants. BUMC's newsletter featured the group prominently with an article, photos, and quotations from graduates, and other employees were invited to participate in the program. The program proved to be effective in improving employee morale and patient satisfaction. "The Sacred Vocation Program is probably the best investment we've made in the last ten years," says BUMC's CEO John McWhorter.[3]

By inviting others to partner with him strategically, Rabbi Samuel Karff chose the path of leading with soul. Because of Samuel Karff's leadership, over a six-year period the Sacred Vocation partnership has helped individual caregivers and their institutions reclaim their sacred vocation, enriching the souls of six institutions and of numerous caregivers and patients.

Conclusion

Medrice Coluccio, Tom Henry, and Rabbi Samuel Karff all found partners to help them choose the path of leading with soul. All three people of deep faith, they shared the conviction that strong inner lives provide the foundation for successful external results. They know that when roots don't receive the nourishment they need, branches eventually wither. They knew that their values could make a difference: in the lives of individual employees, in the lives of customers and patients, and the lives of in organizations.

At the same time, they also shared the conviction that they couldn't blaze a trail of soul-based leadership alone. They knew they needed to stand against a go-it-alone leadership model, risking the disdain of those who would interpret their need for partners as a sign of weakness. They knew they needed to stand with the wisdom of spiritual traditions that teach that souls need one another in order to flourish. By seeking partners, they began to create a community of those yearning to lead from their souls, a community in which a soulful leader is not an oddity, a community in which leading with soul is seen as the *natural* way to lead. By speaking the heart's truth, seeking resonance, and inviting partnerships, they found the partners they needed to begin to bring transformation to organizations and fullness of life to the individuals within them.

Questions

1. How have you spoken your heart's truth in the search for partners?

2. How have you sought resonance among those with whom you have spoken your heart's truth?

3. How have you invited partnerships?

4. What resistance have you encountered, both from within and without, when you have spoken your heart's truth and admitted your need for partners?

Chapter Three

DARING
TO DREAM

I N 2000, the health care picture in the Aswan governorate of
Egypt was bleak. It was common for mothers to die in child-
birth, and twenty-seven out of one thousand infants died before
their first birthday. While the rest of Egypt had made impressive
strides in health care, the mostly rural Aswan region had been left
behind. Low morale, passivity, and lack of commitment were the
norm among health care workers in the region. Despondent and
discouraged, they'd lost hope of ever improving the situation.

Dr. Morsi Mansour, projects coordinator of the Population and
Family Planning Sector of Upper Egypt, had followed his heart to the
Aswan governorate. Recognizing the pressing needs of this troubled
area, he had formed a partnership with Dr. Joan Bragar of Management Sciences for Health in the United States to create a new
leadership program. What was his next step?

Dr. Mansour knew that he needed to dream. Too many years of
despair and despondency had sapped caregivers' energy. Before starting a program or being able to provide useful technical help, he first
of all had to believe in the possibilities.

Daring to dream is part of choosing the path of soul-based leadership. Daring to dream, like following the heart and finding partners, is not always easy — it involves stresses and strains as well as joys and triumphs. This chapter will consider three principles of daring to dream: assessing what is, finding the heart's hope, and dreaming. Each principle will be illustrated with leaders who lived it: Morsi Mansour, The Edge of the rock band U2, and Medrice Coluccio, CEO of St. John Medical Center, introduced in chapter 2.

Assessing What Is

The leader who dares to dream must begin by assessing what is. While many people think of reality as the enemy of dreaming, in fact, hard-headed reality must ground dreaming. While dreaming awakens the inner self in the face of a culture that ignores inner reality, the leader must take external reality into account as a starting point.

MORSI MANSOUR BEGAN by assessing reality. Clear-eyed and unflinching, Morsi examined the situation he faced: low morale, passivity, and despondency, resulting in abysmal health care. With his feet firmly planted on the ground, Morsi took stock. Despite numerous training programs funded by international donors (one program lasted seventy days!), performance had not improved among the health care providers. Convinced that training programs focusing solely on technical skills directed to passively listening health care workers had little effect, Morsi began to seek another way.

THE EDGE, LEAD GUITARIST of the rock band U2, assessed the damage that Hurricane Katrina had inflicted on the music of New Orleans, the city that gave birth to jazz and for many years had served as an incubator for great musicians. Katrina wreaked havoc on New Orleans's music scene, displacing musicians and destroying instruments. With musicians homeless and separated from their bands, their instruments and sound systems damaged or lost, and their performance venues in ruins, it appeared that the New Orleans music scene was irrevocably damaged. Would Hurricane Katrina spell the death of New Orleans jazz and the other music it had spawned? The Edge considered the important role that New Orleans had played in the international music scene:

> It's one of those places in the world where music is such a part of the fabric of the social scene that it's not about a music industry. It's like a music culture exists there, and the entire city is like one giant organic music academy, with grandfathers teaching their grandchildren, brothers showing their brothers how to play. A lot of the traditions are not formalized; they're handed down, so it's a real folk music form. But as it happens, it's also been hugely influential over the decades, in that it became the birthplace of jazz. That form went on to become R & B and funk and rock 'n' roll — any rhythmic music, swing music particularly, dance music, really, you could say — that's probably where it started out.... In terms of New Orleans's long-term identity, long-term contribution to world culture — UNESCO should be taking note of New Orleans.

The Edge considered the tragic possibility that all that New Orleans was contributing to the world music scene would be swept away. The Edge assessed reality and wondered what could be done.

Medrice Coluccio assessed the vital signs of a sick hospital. As she took the pulse of St. John Medical Center, she discovered just how ill her patient was. Looking the cold, hard, facts in the eye, she grasped the bleakness of the hospital's outlook. With its employees' low morale, finances in ruins, and patient satisfaction the worst it had been in years, the hospital teetered on the edge of death. Medrice assessed reality and began to discern how she was called to help.

Finding the Heart's Hope

After assessing reality, the soulful leader finds the heart's hope. Asserting the reality of hope in the face of dire circumstances requires audacious courage. It also requires deep faith in a reality other than the one seen with human eyes. Finding the heart's hope includes drawing on the partnerships one has created and being reminded by one's community of soulful leaders that leading with soul is natural, rather than being a strange concept at odds with the rest of the culture.

MEDRICE COLUCCIO FOUND HER HEART'S HOPE during the interview process as she shared from her heart and saw eyes light up in recognition of what she was seeking to achieve. She found her heart's hope as she listened to the focus groups during the strategic planning process and heard people's stories. She found her heart's hope by getting to know the Sisters of St. Joseph of Peace, by hearing them articulate their call to health care ministry, their mission, their stories of founding the work. She found her heart's hope in her faith, the Roman Catholicism that resonated with the Sisters' faith and told her that God would be with her in her work just as God had been with the Sisters in their work.

THE EDGE FOUND HIS HEART'S HOPE by remembering the music of New Orleans, by being inspired by the power and creativity of the musicians there. He found his heart's hope by noting the resiliency of the musicians who had overcome obstacle after obstacle over the years — obstacles of poverty, racism, and musical snobbery — to establish the musical genres of jazz and blues. He found his heart's hope by remembering the generosity of U2 fans, fans who had already given themselves wholeheartedly to such causes as Amnesty International, Greenpeace, and HIV/AIDS relief in Africa, all causes endorsed by U2. And finally, The Edge found his heart's hope when he toured New Orleans and other Gulf Coast areas, meeting the people themselves, listening to their stories of devastation, and hearing their hopes for restoration and renewal.

D<small>R.</small> M<small>ORSI</small> M<small>ANSOUR</small> <small>FOUND HIS HEART'S HOPE</small> through listening to the people, listening to the caregivers tell the stories of their journey to health care, of the needs they wanted to address. He found his heart's hope when he remembered numerous other times he had thought he was in an impossible situation and a turnaround had occurred. He found his heart's hope learning about his partner Dr. Joan Bragar's empowering leadership model. And finally, he found his heart's hope through his Muslim faith: "If you have faith in God, if your spirit is full of faith, then you will find hope everywhere. You will not give up. It will take patience. There will be obstacles. But you will be like the river, going around the rocks."

Dreaming

After assessing reality and finding the heart's hope, the soulful leader dares to dream. With hope restored, dreams can begin to emerge. Dreams that had begun to fade can return to life, and new dreams can be born. Leaders and their partners dream together, discovering that partnership strengthens hope and multiplies dreams. As they dare to dream together, inner hope and outer partnerships complement one another.

T<small>HE DREAM: HEALTH CARE FOR ALL.</small> Dr. Morsi Mansour dared to dream that a new way was possible. When the head of the Aswan regional health team initially opposed Morsi's efforts to establish a leadership training program, declaring that he refused to have any more ineffectual programs funded by international donors in his governorate, Morsi didn't give up. He went back repeatedly, expressing understanding for the leader's frustration and promising to deliver results in the form of reliable, committed staff. At last the leader, still skeptical, reluctantly approved a short-term pilot program.

With only this grudging permission to move forward, Morsi, undaunted, continued to dream. Furthermore, he showed the Aswan health care workers themselves how they could dare to dream. By inviting the nurses, doctors, and technicians to dream individually and then to share these dreams with one another, Morsi awakened in people long-dormant visions of what health care could be. Although they were reluctant to speak up at first, once the caregivers realized that Morsi believed in them they began to speak from their hearts. Beginning hesitantly in pairs, which soon spread out to the entire group, they poured out their dreams — dreams that every woman in the Aswan region would receive prenatal care, dreams that every infant would be vaccinated. As they spoke about their dreams and discovered that others in the group shared their vision, they began to hope.

Next Morsi and Dr. Joan Bragar worked together to create a leadership training program based on the caregivers' dreams. Beginning in June 2002, this one-year pilot program with a focus on empowerment trained forty-one health care providers from three districts in ten teams. Throughout the program, Morsi and Joan continued to encourage dreaming, sowing seeds of hope. They introduced a "challenge model" of leadership, a simple eight-step model that helped the health care workers think together about how they could realize their dreams by focusing on a measurable result that would take them one step closer to that dream. Participants then took part in a careful assessment of their current situation, and Morsi and Joan helped them formulate a plan for getting from the status quo to where they wanted to be, showing them how to define measurable outcomes with regular measurement toward those outcomes. Morsi and Joan found that once their motivation and hope had been restored, the caregivers easily mastered the technical skills they needed to reach their goals.

The results of the program surprised everyone. Four months into the program, Morsi had already noticed a change in the nurses.

Formerly intimidated by the group environment, the nurses now spoke up frequently and even assumed leadership roles in front of the group. By the end of the program, nurses were conducting training sessions for other health care workers. Furthermore, with their increased confidence, some of the nurses had the courage to speak before high-level health care officials in Cairo, convincing them of the value of the program.

Morale among the health care providers skyrocketed. For most of the participants, taking part in the program was the first opportunity they'd ever had to identify their own challenges and set their own goals, instead of receiving a mandate from someone higher up. With health care workers taking ownership of the vision, teams worked together to achieve their goals. Seventy-five percent of the teams reached 95 percent of their goals in the first year.

Most importantly, when the funding was over in June 2003, the participants said, "We don't need funding. We can do this ourselves." Participants moved into leadership roles and began training health care workers in other districts of the Aswan region. Each of the original ten teams trained several new teams, which in turn trained other teams. Morale improved in the other districts, as did the quality of health care. By mid-2005, over a hundred teams had been trained, making five "generations" of teams. By September of 2005, all of the health care facilities in the Aswan region had been reached by the program, four months ahead of the January 2006 target date.[1]

By the end of 2005, infant mortality in the Aswan region had decreased by 12 percent, and maternal mortality had decreased by 35 percent. Prenatal care and postpartum care also improved dramatically. The formerly pessimistic head of the health team for the Aswan region, who had understandably been reluctant about allowing the leadership development program to proceed, became one of the program's leading advocates. Program graduates spoke of the leadership development program's powerful effect on participants, both within and outside the workplace. As one commented: "I am from the third generation. I was convinced when I saw results happening with the first and second generations of service providers; not only results [at work] but the people themselves changed."[2]

Nagwa Ibrahim Mohamed, a beginning nurse at Gharb Aswan Hospital, testified, "The program showed us how to work properly and to love and help each other."[3]

The self-run program continues to this day and continues to succeed. Empowerment, leadership skills, and dreaming have proven effective in Aswan. Furthermore, other parts of the world have turned to the Aswan project as a role model. Aswan's leadership development program is serving as a paradigm for other parts of Egypt and the developing world.

Morsi Mansour dared to dream, and by teaching others to do the same has helped to effect a transformation of health care in the Aswan governorate and even throughout Egypt and the rest of the world.

THE DREAM: RESTORING THE MUSIC OF NEW ORLEANS. The Edge also dared to dream. His dream was that the music of New Orleans could be restored. He formed a partnership with well-known producer Bob Ezrin and Henry Juszkiewicz, CEO of Gibson Guitar. Pooling their influence, skills, and contacts, the three began to build a network. They dreamed that members of the music industry, so often in competition, could come together for a worthy cause, and they invited all who were involved in the industry, from musicians to instrument manufacturers to promoters, to participate. As they shared their vision with one another and brainstormed possible names, Henry's press officer, Caroline Galloway, suggested "Music Rising," and The Edge and Bob exclaimed, "That's it!" They adopted the slogan "Rebuilding the Gulf Coast, note by note" from a slogan they had seen written as graffiti and on T-shirts around New Orleans: "Rebuilding New Orleans, note by note." The logo, designed by Bill Cathcart, followed: a musical note nested between phoenix wings flapping and rising.

In late 2005, The Edge visited New Orleans and other Gulf Coast cities, talking to musicians and helping them envision how their music could rise again. As he met musicians whose instruments had been lost or damaged, as he learned about their needs, he invited each musician to dream with him about what was possible. The result? Music Rising agreed to give each qualified musician $1,000 to purchase an instrument and the gear to go with it. Furthermore, MusiCares, a partner nonprofit that had signed on to distribute the grants, was able, through a special arrangement with the online equipment store Musiciansfriend, to make the instruments available to the musicians at wholesale prices. In April 2006, The Edge, Henry, and Bob helped reopen Preservation Hall in New Orleans and presented new instruments to the Preservation Jazz Band. The next day The Edge and the Music Rising team toured the Lower 9th Ward and, stunned by how little had changed in the four months since The Edge's previous visit, vowed to redouble their aid efforts. Moved by the courageous role that churches play in the community, The Edge announced soon thereafter that Music Rising's Phase II would also donate instruments to churches and schools whose music programs had been decimated by Katrina.

Music Rising raises money through donations, auctions, benefit concerts, and sales of a specially designed Gibson guitar that has wood from New Orleans and other Gulf Coast areas replacing the usual plastic scratch plate of the instrument. An online ticket auction held throughout the month of April 2006 involved sixty artists working alongside Ticketmaster and other promoters. Fans bid on tickets to more than eighty concerts and also bid on special Gibson guitars, autographed by participating musicians, that had been donated for the cause. Artists were quick to support the effort, and Ticketmaster donated all of its service fees. The auction raised substantial funds and dramatically increased awareness of the need. In June 2006, Music Rising received the Halo Award from the Cause Marketing Forum at its annual conference in New York. Designed to recognize the good that can be accomplished when businesses and nonprofits partner, the award was given to Music Rising for its effective fundraising and marketing campaign.

In September 2006, Music Rising hosted the reopening of the New Orleans Superdome. Fulfilling a dream born half a year previously on the night before the Grammy awards, U2 and Green Day performed "The Saints Are Coming" together at the NFL pre-game show, lending their support to the rebirth of the city.

Music Rising's biggest fundraising event, an April 2007 "Icons of Music" auction in New York, raised $2.5 million. Auction items included The Edge's 1975 cream Gibson Les Paul custom guitar, which he had played on every U2 tour since 1985 (it sold for $240,000). The Edge and the other U2 band members agreed that they would donate items to the auction that were difficult for them to part with, and encouraged musicians from other bands to donate sacrificially as well. The Edge mused:

> I thought there was some poetry in putting up an instrument that really meant something to me, that wasn't just something I had in the back cupboard, for the city, because the city's given me, and so many other musicians like me, so much. Really, without New Orleans, there would be no rock 'n' roll. So I just felt it was right and proper to really stump up with something that was of significant value, something that meant a lot to me. So that was the instrument that I thought was the right choice.

The results of Music Rising's efforts? Over twenty-five hundred professional musicians have been reestablished, and thirty thousand students and residents of Orleans Parish have been aided. Twenty-one school music programs and forty-one church music programs are back on their feet. The Edge reflected:

> It's been very gratifying to start seeing some photographs coming in from the different schools, showing their music classes

and getting a sense of what this has meant on the ground. It's an incredible thing to put a musical instrument in the hands of a kid. It's a really life-changing thing, and I think particularly in a city like New Orleans, where the prospects are maybe not as rosy as they might be in other cities in the United States, not only is it a way of giving children a goal and a focus for their life, but it's also an opportunity for them to really learn to do something that will put food on the table.

Perhaps most remarkable of all, competing factions of the music industry have demonstrated unprecedented cooperation. In The Edge's view:

> In some ways, I was pushing an open door. It was remarkable how, once we had formalized things and put a structure on a way of trying to help, people came on board and were willing to become part of this idea. It's much more of a testimony, I think, to the power of the music of New Orleans and the importance of it than it is to my ability to motivate people or Bob Ezrin's ability to motivate people, or anyone else involved. I think we just happened to be in the lucky position of having the wherewithal to actually get something going.

Not only have musicians and music programs been reestablished, but also hope is returning to the city through the restoration of the music. It was as if the music restored the soul of the city. The Edge observed:

> The first time we actually got to New Orleans after we'd been able to put some professional musicians back to work, we were struck by the fact that music is not just a cultural identity issue in New Orleans — it's part of what drives the city. . . . Whenever the music was playing, there was a sense of optimism about the future, a sense of "this can work." It became a great catalyst; I think that a lot of the music-based initiatives have fed the

soul of the city in a way that I don't think people fully got initially.... That was totally unforeseen by Bob, Henry, and me, and when we figured that out, it was an amazing moment, to realize that it was like unlocking people's faith for the future.

In August 2007, two years after Katrina, Music Rising assessed the progress in New Orleans and recommitted to its relief efforts. The Edge stated:

On this second anniversary of the Katrina disaster it's apparent that we still have much to do. We will continue to support and stay focused on the needs of the musicians, schools and churches.[4]

Reflecting on the role of Music Rising in his own life, The Edge maintains that the initiative has nurtured his soul. While he has given a great deal to Music Rising, the project has given even more back to him:

It's been an amazingly rewarding thing. I have to say that whatever time and money and effort I've put into Music Rising personally, I've been repaid tenfold in terms of just the thrill and reward of realizing that this has actually made a significant difference. So I count it as much more of a blessing than anything else. It's something that's enriched my life, rather than something that's been a labor.

THE DREAM: A THRIVING HOSPITAL. Medrice Coluccio dared to dream, not only with the focus groups and strategic planning team as discussed in chapter 2, but also with the implementation team she put together after the strategic plan had been adopted by the board. Just as she had invited the focus groups to dream by asking the question, "If you could wave your magic wand, what would you like to see different come out of our health care ministry here?" and just as she had dared to dream with the strategic planning team that they could create a realistic and achievable plan, so she dared to dream with the implementation team that the sick hospital could recover in five years.

The implementation team, with its unconventional "champions," outlined nine strategic initiatives, each led by one of the champions. Each of the strategic initiatives invited people from across the hospital system to dream:

> Weaving mission and values
> Developing our leaders
> Improving our facilities
> Being excellent stewards
> Showcasing our excellent physicians
> Enhancing our service continuum
> Providing service excellence
> Creating pride and loyalty
> Telling our story

Medrice, a former circuit tennis player, reminded teams to keep their eyes on the ball as they reached for their dreams in each area.

What was the outcome of dreaming together? The results astonished everyone. During her interview process for the position of CEO, Coluccio had noticed that people referred to St. John Medical Center as a "stepsister" in the PeaceHealth system. She had responded, "No one should have to be a stepsister to anyone." Three and a half years later, when the CEO of the entire PeaceHealth system gathered everyone together and gave out systemwide awards, St. John won in every category. The hospital received the Stewardship Award for its financial health, the Pride and Loyalty Award, the Creativity Award, and the Quality Award. Reflecting on the occasion, Coluccio remembers how she felt as St. John received award after award. "It was getting embarrassing, but then it was actually kind of fun. It was really gratifying for people at St. John to be recognized for their good work."

What was the good work that earned these awards? The improvements were numerous. By the end of its third year, 92 percent of the dreams articulated in the five-year strategic plan had been achieved. For example, St. John had spearheaded the development of a free clinic staffed by volunteer physicians, nurses, mental health professionals, and other staff, which opened in late 2005. Serving the growing uninsured population in the Longview area, the clinic provided free urgent care and improved access to ongoing care.

St. John also upgraded its facilities and equipment. The hospital added such leading-edge technology as Cat Scan and MRI equipment, and state-of-the-art cancer diagnosis and radiation treatment equipment, thus offering technology close to home that was equal to or better than what could be found in the nearest major cities, allowing more patients to find what they needed locally. Furthermore, a $46 million project oversaw renovation of all eight floors of the hospital, including the construction of a new family-friendly birthing center, an expanded critical-care unit, an improved emergency department, and technology-enhanced surgical and cardiology floors.

Staff morale had improved tremendously. When Coluccio arrived, the feeling among staff members was, in her words, "deflated — the confidence wasn't there." St. John had suffered from high turnover and absenteeism, and 17 percent of its employees were temporary agency personnel. By the end of 2005, turnover and absenteeism had been reduced to very low levels. The hospital was finding it easy to recruit new employees, and no agency personnel were needed. St. John was also offering training opportunities to its staff. In its commitment to ongoing leadership training, the hospital offered tuition remission to its employees for undergraduate and graduate coursework, as well as funds for continuing education. Internally, St. John offered a comprehensive orientation program and ongoing competency training. A mission-based leadership training program was offered to middle and senior management.

Patient satisfaction had increased, and the hospital's image in the community had turned around dramatically. A number of new programs had improved patient care and patient satisfaction. For example, St. John participated in the "Speak Up!" program, a national effort to improve patient safety.[5] Based on research which shows that patients who take part in decisions about their health care are more likely to have better outcomes, the "Speak Up!" program encourages patients to become active participants in their own care.

In another significant hospital improvement, critical-care nurses, respiratory therapists, and physicians worked together to reduce the number of ventilator-associated pneumonia cases. At the 2004 Washington State Quality Conference, St. John received a Certificate of Merit for Infection Control and Prevention for reducing its ventilator-associated pneumonia rate to 1 percent, far below the national average (and down from 17 percent at St. John in the late 1990s).

The hospital's community image has improved, not only because of improved patient satisfaction, but also because of the significant ways St. John has given back to the community. In addition to the free clinic mentioned above, St. John has also given to the community by sponsoring a youth mentorship program for at-risk youth, underwriting patient assistance programs, and offering financial gifts. The youth mentorship program, conceived by Sr. Rose Marie Nigro (champion of the "Weave mission and values into our organizational fabric" strategic initiative) as a response to the high dropout rate among area high school students, has offered at-risk juniors and seniors financial assistance to attend college, as well as coaching to help them succeed academically. The hospital's patient assistance program for uninsured and underinsured patients includes debt financing for patients who can't qualify for loans, grants through an internal charity program, and services to assist patients in applying for the sliding scale, income-based state health plan. St. John's financial contributions to the community, totaling nearly $100,000 in 2005, included donations to an emergency shelter, the United Way, and arts programs including a local theater, as well as closely related organizations such as the American Cancer Society, the March of Dimes, and the Red Cross.

Finally, the hospital is now flourishing financially. When Medrice Coluccio arrived, St. John was operating severely in the red. By the end of 2005, the hospital was operating in the black, far exceeding its financial targets. The ratio of income to expense went from −3 percent to 8 percent in three years. In 2005, as noted above, this remarkable financial recovery won St. John the Peace Health systemwide Stewardship Award.

All along the way, the hospital implementation team committed itself to communicating progress on the strategic initiative dreams to all stakeholders. In order to communicate progress, the team needed to know what it was measuring. The implementation team understood that daring to dream and down-to-earth measurement go together. For some strategic initiatives, data collection and the tools to measure the data were already in place. For example, the strategic initiative "Improve our facilities" had articulated as one of its goals "Make the physical organization easy to navigate." Once they had posted new signage and assigned volunteer "ambassadors" to assist patients and families in finding their way, the team knew it had achieved its goal. Likewise, the strategic initiative "Be excellent stewards of our resources" had named the goal "Improve the revenue stream." When the ratio of income to expenses went from −3 percent to 8 percent, they knew they had achieved their goal.

Other goals weren't as easy to measure. How, for example, could "Create pride and loyalty" or "Weave mission and values into our organizational fabric" be measured? Convinced that only that which can be measured is ultimately seen as valued, St. John leaders knew that they needed to be able to measure changes in the health of the organization as the dreams that made up their mission-based strategic plan fell into place. They decided to utilize pioneering measurement tools developed by Bill Mahoney of the Peace Health Center for Mission to measure how well the hospital was attaining its "soft" goals.

These tools measure organizational health by examining (1) how engaged in their work caregivers are, (2) how the sense of "teamness" functions in the work units and departments, and (3) how engaging the culture is. For example, the "teamness" survey asks respondents to give a score to such statements as "In my work unit we nurture, support, and care for one another," "In my work unit we handle conflicts in a calm, caring, and healing manner," and "Regardless of the topic, communication between the people in my work unit is direct, truthful, respectful, and positive." The survey measuring how engaging the culture is includes such statements as "I am provided the opportunity to learn and grow in my current job," "The work I do is valued by the other people in my department," and "I am allowed to use my unique personal skills and abilities for the benefit of patients and co-workers." Among the statements included in the survey measuring caregivers' level of engagement in their work are "I often talk with other employees at St. John about what caring and healing means and how it can be achieved," "The work I do has a clear impact on supporting the healing of patients," and "I have a personal vision of what patient care at St. John could be."

St. John administered the surveys every year beginning in 2002. Using the 2002 data as a baseline, the hospital's organizational health scores showed statistically significant improvement in three out of the four subsequent years. These measurements demonstrated that dreaming together and partnering to achieve goals had made a significant impact on organizational health.

Thus, by discovering how to measure progress toward "soft" goals as well as progress toward hard goals, St. John focused on the impact of its entire strategic plan, rather than just part of it. The hospital's organizational health, as well as its financial bottom line, could be seen and valued.

In addition to St. John Medical Center's marked improvement in employee morale, financial health, and patient satisfaction three years into its five-year strategic plan, the financial health of the hospital was contributing to the economic health of the larger community. Most importantly, enthusiasm for meeting the strategic goals remained high, and increasing numbers of stakeholders were becoming engaged with the process.

Medrice Coluccio received the Catholic Health Association's 2006 Midcareer Leadership award for daring to dream that things could be different at St. John Medical Center. CHA honored the "passion, work, and friendship" that helped revitalize St. John. At the awards ceremony, Coluccio was recognized as a leader whose "compassionate guidance is at once an example of what we are about and a promise for our future."

By daring to dream, Medrice Coluccio demonstrated that turn-arounds are possible, even in the most dire circumstances. In just three and a half years, morale had skyrocketed, patient satisfaction improved dramatically, and the financial situation had turned around. The hospital on a respirator was restored to full health and was fully serving the community.

Conclusion

Morsi Mansour, The Edge, and Medrice Coluccio all dared to dream when they faced "impossible" challenges. Far from denying reality, they assessed reality squarely. They balanced external reality with internal strength and asserted the reality of hope in the face of despair. They found their hearts' hope through connecting with others, knowing they needed to draw on the community of partners they had created in order that their hope could flourish. They found their hearts' hope through remembering other times when hope had overcome despair. And they found their hearts' hope through their faith. They dared to dream, against all odds, that change was possible. They demonstrated the power of dreaming and then, through tapping into their souls' strength, moved from dream to reality. Others found their dreams contagious and stepped out to join them, with remarkable results.

Questions

1. How have you assessed "what is" when facing challenges?

2. How have you found your heart's hope? How might you find your heart's hope in a current challenge you are facing?

3. How have you dared to dream?

4. How might you dare to dream now?

PART TWO

STAYING ON TRACK

Chapter Four

KEEPING MISSION AT THE FORE

I N THE EARLY 1990S, Bob Glassman, cofounder and cochairman of Wainwright Bank in Boston, found himself in a challenging situation. A few years earlier, the bank had dared to dream by beginning to experiment with social justice projects, most notably forming a partnership with the Pine Street Inn shelter to address homelessness. Although Bob was committed to a vision of social justice for the bank, he realized that not everybody on the bank's board shared his vision. While they were willing to tolerate a smaller experiment, a serious, ongoing commitment to social justice was unheard of for a bank. Concerned about the values vacuum at the center of the banking industry, Bob puzzled over how the bank could stay true to its motto of "Banking on Values."

Keeping mission at the fore is a fundamental element of staying on track with soul-based leadership. Keeping mission at the fore, like following the heart, finding partners, and daring to dream, involves many ups and downs. This chapter will consider three principles of keeping mission at the fore: focusing on something more, sharing the vision, and returning to mission. Each principle will be illustrated by examples from the lives of leaders who lived it: Bob Glassman,

Anita Roddick, founder of the Body Shop, and Jim Sanger, CEO of St. Mary's Good Samaritan Hospitals in southern Illinois.

Focusing on Something More

Bob Glassman focused on something more than the bottom line. In a banking world known for its focus on the single bottom line of profitability, Wainwright Bank became known, first, for its double bottom line, focusing on both people and profits, and then, later, for its triple bottom line, focusing on people, profits, and the planet. In order to focus on the bigger picture, Bob took small steps, beginning by talking with his business partner in the early 1990s. When Bob told his partner he'd like the bank to pursue his vision of social justice, his partner pledged his full support.

ONE OF ANITA RODDICK'S FAVORITE SAYINGS inspired her work every day: "If you think you're too small to have an impact, try going to bed with a mosquito." At the beginning, Anita Roddick may have identified with a mosquito buzzing around big business while it tried to sleep, but by her untimely death in 2007 she was a force to be reckoned with. She left a rich legacy, leading with soul both at the Body Shop, the company she founded, and throughout the world through leaders she influenced.

In all that she did, Anita Roddick stayed on track by focusing on something more than the bottom line. From her first Body Shop, a tiny store in Brighton, England, which she opened in 1976 in order to ensure her family's survival, to the business she sold for millions in 2006 (immediately turning the profits over to a charitable foundation), Roddick focused on her vision and values — above all, respect for people and care for the environment.[1]

JIM SANGER FELT DRAWN to St. Mary's Good Samaritan Hospitals in southern Illinois because of the group's focus on something more than the bottom line. Jim wanted to focus on health care as a ministry serving the community, and he was attracted to leadership within a religiously affiliated health care institution. With its Franciscan Catholic heritage and its focus on mission, vision, and values, St. Mary's Good Samaritan fit the bill.

St. Mary's Good Samaritan articulates its mission thus:

To continue the healing ministry of Jesus Christ by improving and providing regional, cost-effective quality health services for everyone, with a special concern for the poor and vulnerable.

Expanding upon the mission stated above, St. Mary's Good Samaritan enumerates its values:

As partners in the healing ministry, we are committed to:

- Providing compassionate and competent service
- Acting justly
- Respecting the dignity of all
- Fostering a spirit of community

In all that he does as CEO of St. Mary's Good Samaritan, Jim Sanger focuses on more than the bottom line, always keeping his eye on the greater good.

Sharing the Vision

Jim Sanger recognizes that shared vision lies at the foundation of St. Mary's Good Samaritan's success. When Jim arrived as CEO in 1997, charged with merging the leadership of two hospitals that had recently entered into a joint operating agreement, he knew he faced a tough challenge. While teamwork functioned well in subunits of the two hospitals, the leadership team lacked a shared vision.[2]

Aware of the pitfalls of merging two management teams, Jim started by treating everyone with dignity and respect and expecting everyone else to do the same. He announced that one management team, not two, would lead St. Mary's Good Samaritan. He then gave each member of the management team responsibilities at both campuses, requiring each one to set foot on the unfamiliar campus and get to know the needs there. Through (1) the stated expectation that the team would work together, and (2) annual retreats in which people not only worked together but also socialized together, the management team gradually consolidated. The hospitals committed to a no-layoff policy: whenever someone in a management position would leave either campus, the position was merged with the parallel position from the other campus.

Concurrent with the merging of leadership, Jim worked with all levels of leadership and management to develop a shared vision. He invested time, energy, and money in the task, and he stood steady as the forces of change whirled around him. By 2007, ten years after his arrival, the entire leadership team shared the same vision. The institution now functions powerfully, successfully meeting its goals. In Jim's view:

> The essence of getting an organization to be successful and to go in a good direction is having a nucleus of people who understand the vision. It's that team learning, that shared mental model, that shared vision. If that truly exists, most of the decisions that will be made throughout the course of a day or a week or a month or a year will be the right ones. If you have enough people, that critical mass, who get it, things get a lot easier because it's not a whole series of disconnected decisions that are being driven by the moment. It's more a series of connected decisions made by people who all want to get to a certain place.

With shared vision, Jim has discovered, anything is possible.

ANITA RODDICK SHARED VISION INFECTIOUSLY. Her husband, Gordon, caught her vision early on, and they became partners a year after Anita had opened her business, operating the first two Body Shops in Brighton and Chichester. Soon after, friends and customers began asking if they could open Body Shops, and Gordon, who had never heard of franchising, "invented" the concept. Anita interviewed everyone who was interested in opening a shop, asking questions that drilled down to vision and values. Most of the new shops were run by women who caught and contributed to the vision. Reflecting back on the Body Shop's development, Anita mused:

> The Body Shop is not, and nor was ever, a one-woman-show —
> it's a global operation with thousands of people working toward
> common goals and sharing common values. That's what has
> given it a campaigning and commercial strength and continues
> to set it apart from mainstream business.[3]

Like Jim Sanger, Anita had discovered that the power of a vision increases exponentially when the vision is shared.

BOB GLASSMAN WORKED TO DEVELOP shared vision at Wainwright Bank. In the early 1990s, with his partner's full support of a social justice vision for the bank, he turned to board development. When Bob clarified his vision for the direction of the bank, he found that some board members' eyes lit up and others' shut down. Some self-selected off the board, while new members who shared Bob's vision for the bank joined the board.

Bob also sought to develop shared vision among the members of the bank's management team. As some managers caught the vision and as new managers joined the bank for its vision, an inner core of board members and managers who shared the vision solidified. Bob reflected:

And this inner core would constantly talk, and out of those conversations we had ideas we would put into place. We were assisted by the fact that we didn't have to push the agenda out on the public. We felt we had something that was right and as the public learned about it, one person at a time, they would assimilate who we were and what we were doing. We created an identity for the bank. When that developed, there was a passionate, committed constituency that found its way here. Then that created another cycle of enthusiasm to take it a step further.

In time, the board articulated Wainwright Bank's mission:

With a sense of inclusion and diversity that extends from the mailroom to the boardroom, Wainwright Bank and Trust Company resolves to be a leading socially responsible bank. The Bank is equally committed to all its stakeholders — employees, customers, communities, and shareholders.

The shared vision became the rallying point for recruiting new board members and new employees, and also guided decisions about product development and employee policies.

Returning to Mission

Again and again, Bob Glassman returned to his vision of social justice as a mission for Wainwright Bank. As he sought to take small steps toward putting the mission into practice, he returned to the vision regularly for inspiration and guidance. In the early days, for example, the vision served as his compass whenever a new product was launched or an annual report was written: "Utilizing every platform available to the bank, including speaking engagements, annual reports, newsletters, product brochures, and print ads, there was a subtext, and the heart of that message was always our commitment to social justice." By 2007, twenty years after the bank's founding, Wainwright Bank boasted numerous products that manifested its mission. The bank provides loans to underserved groups, including loans for affordable housing, homeless shelters, food banks, environmental protection, health centers, HIV/AIDS services, and immigration services. It also offers "Green Loans," loans with reduced interest rates for energy-efficient buildings.

Wainwright Bank has become the market leader for the nonprofit world. By paying attention to an area that other banks didn't address, Wainwright Bank developed a cultural fluency for lending to nonprofits, learning the complex lending laws and understanding the particular needs of the nonprofit world. Furthermore, Wainwright Bank provides investment opportunities in line with its mission. Along with other socially responsible CDs, Wainwright Bank offers customers the option to invest in Equal Exchange CDs, which support coffee farmers in developing countries. In addition, *CommunityRoom.net,* a Web-site-hosting service provided to all nonprofits holding Wainwright Bank accounts, generates over $1 million in donations to the nonprofits annually. Second, in addition to providing products and services that manifest the mission, Wainwright Bank manifests the mission within the company. In the last several years, branches have been "going green."

The bank hires with an eye toward diversity. Reflecting on the early years, Bob Glassman remarks: "I wanted Human Resources to make every attempt in all sectors of the bank to reach out and have the employee base as much as possible reflect the community we serve, which in turn enabled us to get the best possible people." That commitment earned the bank a reputation. Now Wainwright Bank has a waiting list of people who contact Human Resources from other banks in town, saying they'd love to work at Wainwright. Wainwright Bank hires inclusively, not discriminating with regard to race, gender, ethnicity, or sexual orientation. Sixty percent of Wainwright Bank's employees and nearly 50 percent of the bank's officers are women. Over 30 percent of the bank's employees are minorities, and employees speak twenty-two languages. The bank was one of the earliest to provide domestic part- ner benefits, leading the way in the banking industry. Bob Glassman's persistent focus on mission has paid off, financially as well as socially. Naysayers assumed that Wainwright Bank would suffer financially for its idealism, claiming that loans for homeless shelters and food banks are risky business. In fact, the opposite is true: Wainwright Bank's $700 million in community development loans has experienced zero losses over the twenty years of the bank's life, in sharp contrast to other banks' loan portfolios. Bob Glassman reflects:

> There's a kind of tenacity, if I can call it moral tenacity [among borrowers], to stick with it and see it through because they come to the project . . . working for a cause. We've found they're able to work through any bumps along the road. It's been a terrific piece of moral collateral that's just not present in other lending.[4]

Furthermore, Wainwright Bank has grown steadily over the past twenty years, with, for example, $300 million in deposits in 1997 and over $900 million in 2007 In 2006, loans increased 9 percent over 2005, and net interest income was $27.6 million, up from $26.9 million in 2005. Now boasting twelve branches in the Bos- ton area, Wainwright Bank is among the seven hundred largest of the eight thousand banks in the United States. Bob Glassman dreams that Wainwright Bank will continue to inspire socially responsible behavior:

> I'd like more people to learn about what we do, and to under- stand that their money is going to do something. The choice they are making to put it in Place A or Place B has social consequences for the community. I think they ought to think about that. I think the investment community needs to think about that.

While Bob doesn't aspire to transform the banking industry, he hopes that a significant percentage of the population will catch on to his vision for what is possible when their banking reflects their values.

Linda Cornell, president/CEO of the Visiting Nurse Association of Eastern Massachusetts, testifies to what Wainwright Bank his meant to her organization: "Wainwright Bank has been the epitome of the community bank — very socially responsible. We were a little community organization with a big dream, and they believed in us. They financed the dream and made it happen."[5]

Jim O'Connell, of Boston Healthcare for the Homeless, reflects on his organization's relationship with Wainwright: "You can imagine our shock when we went to Wainwright Bank, and they actually courted us. They wanted our business. Nobody wants our business."[6]

Wainwright's loan will help Boston Healthcare for the Homeless renovate a former morgue and turn it into a health care facility for the homeless. In 2007, *American Banker* named Bob Glassman one of its 2007 Community Bankers of the Year. Likened by those in the banking industry to an Oscar, this award raised Wainwright's profile and celebrated the success of Wainwright's unconventional approach. By keeping mission at the fore, Bob Glassman has demonstrated, against the banking industry's conventional wisdom, that social conscience and profitability can mutually support one another.

ANITA RODDICK ALSO KEPT MISSION at the fore, returning to it regularly at the Body Shop. The company's mission was articulated early on, as shown on the following page. the Body Shop also committed itself to developing its products without the use of animal testing.

Returning to the mission helped Anita assess which products, which suppliers, and which employment practices fit with the Body Shop's identity. With a quickly growing company made up of many different franchise owners, it would have been easy for Anita to give in to conventional business wisdom and become a leader focused on the single bottom line. But Anita resisted the pressure. She remained

THE BODY SHOP MISSION STATEMENT

- To dedicate our business to the pursuit of social and environmental change

- To creatively balance the financial and human needs of our stakeholders: employees, customers, franchisees, suppliers, and shareholders

- To courageously ensure that our business is ecologically sustainable, meeting the needs of the present without compromising the future

- To meaningfully contribute to local, national, and international communities in which we trade, by adopting a code of conduct which ensures care, honesty, fairness, and respect[7]

committed to leading with soul, and stayed on track by keeping her eye on the mission.

For example, in the areas of product development and choice of suppliers, Anita created a community trade program to help fulfill the fourth tenet of the company's mission ("to meaningfully contribute to local, national, and international communities in which we trade"). The community trade program, the Body Shop's approach to fair trade, grew out of Anita's international travels and the partnerships she formed in the 1980s. As she traveled, Anita noticed both the crying needs in disadvantaged communities and the rich resources the people had to offer. She offered these communities opportunities for economic development by supplying natural ingredients and accessories to the Body Shop. Now with over thirty-five suppliers from twenty-five countries, the Body Shop has been contributing to economic development for people in need for over twenty years. From sesame oil from Nicaragua to marula oil from Namibia, natural ingredients from disadvantaged communities have been mainstreamed into Body Shop products.[8]

Anita discovered that practicing fair trade had many challenges, and she came to understand why those who had tried it hadn't always stayed the course. Small suppliers sometimes were unable to fulfill large orders consistently, local organizations didn't always treat the local people with dignity and respect, and the Body Shop's environmental standards and standards for animal protection were not always upheld. Not to be dissuaded, in 1994 Anita and other Body Shop leaders created the Body Shop's Fair Trade Guidelines to ensure that it chose its suppliers in a manner consistent with the company's mission:

- COMMUNITY: We are looking to work with established community organizations which represent the interests of their people.

- COMMUNITY IN NEED: We target those groups who are disadvantaged in some way, those whose opportunities are limited.

- BENEFITS: We want the primary producers and their wider community to benefit from the trade — socially as well as economically.

- COMMERCIAL VIABILITY: It has to make good commercial sense, meaning that price, quality, capacity, and availability are carefully considered.

- ENVIRONMENTAL SUSTAINABILITY: The trade has to meet the Body Shop standards for environmental and animal protection.[9]

Not only does the Body Shop utilize these standards in choosing new partners, it now also uses them regularly to evaluate existing partnerships. Furthermore, the company works closely with alternative trade organizations such as OXFAM and TWIN trading in order to benefit from their fair-trade expertise.

Anita viewed the community trade program as a means to further all aspects of the Body Shop's mission. For Anita, commerce at its best was about much more than money:

> Our trade with these communities is not just about creating another product or market for the Body Shop. It is about exchange and value, trade and respect, friendship and trust.[10]

In addition to the community trade program, Anita returned to the mission in her initiative to activate self-esteem. Despising the way the cosmetics industry played on women's insecurities, she focused on building women's self-esteem. In her advertising and product development, Anita took a different approach from that taken by the traditional cosmetics industry. She helped women focus on valuing and caring for both their bodies and their souls.

For example, the Body Shop promises, "We will not promise eternal youth, or prey on people's insecurities, but focus instead on products that provide well-being and comfort." The Body Shop educates its customers by communicating honestly and clearly on its labels, avoiding misleading claims, and telling customers exactly what is in its products and what the products will do. The Body Shop's motto, "Know your mind, love your body," is lived out in all its product communications.[11]

In 1997, the Body Shop created Ruby, a doll representing real women, with the caption "There are three billion women in the world who don't look like supermodels and only eight who do." The Body Shop launched a campaign based on Ruby to help promote self-esteem.[12]

In addition, as part of the self-esteem initiative, Anita championed stopping violence against women, using her shops to raise awareness of the issue and to link women to resources that could help them stop the cycle of violence.

Through these and many other initiatives, Anita Roddick demonstrated to the world that capitalism, even capitalism devoted to beauty and health products, could have a soul. Through the phenomenal growth of the Body Shop, she put forth a vision of what business could be. Because of Anita Roddick, the sleeping world of business has been buzzed repeatedly by a mosquito and has been awakened to greater possibilities.[13]

JIM SANGER RETURNED TO MISSION again and again in his efforts to merge the leadership of the two hospitals, St. Mary's and Good Samaritan. While the mission gets lived out regularly in daily life at St. Mary's Good Samaritan in such things as opening meetings with prayer, having Sisters on the board, and requiring that executives drive simple cars, it also has implications in the nuts-and-bolts of such things as budgeting. For example, when Jim arrived in 1997, he drew attention to the capital budget and asked, "Is the organization's capital budget being spent in a manner consistent with its vision?" After examining the capital budget, the leadership team's answer was "No." So Jim and others decided to rearrange spending priorities, agreeing that at least 60 percent of the budget should be strategic. Periodically, they reviewed the budget to see whether it was achieving what the hospitals' mission and vision statements said they wanted to achieve. When the hospitals weren't achieving their stated goals, they readjusted the budget. Within two years, the budget had been readjusted significantly, and the hospitals were back on track, successfully achieving more of their goals. Furthermore, every year when he develops the capital budget for the year ahead, Jim returns to the mission:

> Every year, we articulate the strategic plan, and then we talk about how we will get it done. We also discuss how the capital plan will support the strategic plan. For instance, more recently, strategic capital has been shifted to support operations. This was in response to the concern that we had declared patient satisfaction as a major initiative and had failed to provide the resources to pursue patient satisfaction at a high level. We modified the

budget to provide more resources to support this important initiative.

Besides regularly returning to the mission in decisions about capital allocation, Jim also returns to the mission in his own reflection time. Most weekends, Jim takes time to step back and look at the big picture, asking, "Where did we go this week, and is that where we intended to go?" He keeps his eye on the company's vision and tries "to stay out of the busy work, the detail, the crises that constantly try to redirect an organization." Jim knows from experience how easily a leader can get sidetracked and emphasizes, "The day-to-day things you have to deal with cannot be allowed to take over the driving of the organization." He keeps a master list of the things the hospitals are committed to working on in order to achieve their mission, and he reviews that list most weekends, "so when I come in on a Monday morning, I know where I want to go that week." Jim also assists each member of his leadership team in doing the same kind of reflection.

Conclusion

Bob Glassman, Anita Roddick, and Jim Sanger all kept mission at the fore when challenges arose that threatened to throw them off track. They focused on something more than the bottom line, developed shared vision, and repeatedly returned to mission. In the midst of the day-to-day crises that threatened to pull their organizations away from their vision, they kept their focus on the big picture. By keeping mission at the fore they kept reminding themselves, their employees, and their customers and patients of their raison d'être. Through thick and thin, they stayed on track, inspired their employees, and built strong organizations that knew where they were going and consistently achieved their goals.

Queries

1. How have you focused on *something more?*

2. How have you developed shared vision?

3. How might you develop shared vision in a current challenge you are facing?

4. How have you returned to mission? How might you return to mission in a current challenge?

Chapter Five

PRACTICING GRATITUDE

I N THE EARLY 1990S, Landry's Bicycles (introduced in chapter 2) faced a major crisis. The company had opened its new store six months later than planned, causing Landry's to miss out on a significant part of its projected seasonal business. With the expenses of a new store, low revenues, an economic recession, and the rent due, the bank pulled Landry's loan and advised the company to file for bankruptcy. Struggling for survival and seeking a way forward, manager Tom Henry presented this apparently impossible challenge to a roundtable gathering of the support group for business leaders, Seeing Things Whole, to which he belonged. As the group struggled under the burden of the Landrys' situation, a member of the roundtable asked a surprising question: "How might you see your work as a gift rather than as a burden?"

Keeping mission at the fore, which is fundamental to staying on track, strengthens the leader's soul and the soul of the organization. Practicing gratitude, the theme of this chapter, complements the focus on mission. By practicing gratitude, leaders can stay on track themselves and can help keep their organizations on track. Three principles are at the core of practicing gratitude: receiving work (and colleagues) as gift, pioneering practices of gratitude, and creating a culture of gratitude. This chapter will explore each of these principles in turn, illustrating them with examples from of the lives of leaders who lived it: Tom Henry, Meg Clapp, director of the MGH pharmacy (introduced in chapter 1), and Tom Grant, former CEO of LabOne, a laboratory in Kansas City that analyzed specimens for the medical profession.

Receiving Work (and Colleagues) as Gift

The struggle for gratitude and appreciation is universal. Every human being feels overworked and underappreciated at times. Likewise, everyone, in the press of busyness and stress, forgets to thank those whose work makes theirs possible.

The roundtable member's question changed everything for Tom Henry. Despite the seeming impossibility of the situation faced by Landry's, Tom began to find ways to view his work as gift rather than burden. And he preached that message to his co-workers at Landry's.

With this shift in perspective, Tom found new hope to face his challenges. Once, after the bank pulled its loan, Landry's needed $40,000 immediately in order to avoid bankruptcy. Because he was viewing the opportunity to work at Landry's as a gift and because he believed in the possibilities of Landry's, Tom branched out to other sources of financing, approaching friends for loans. He didn't feel guilty doing so because he genuinely believed it was a way of sharing his enthusiasm for the good work Landry's was doing. And his belief was infectious. An artist friend lent Landry's $5,000 from his savings, even though he was far from wealthy. Another friend sold stock he had inherited from his parents to provide another $5,000 loan. Fairly quickly, with small loans from various supporters, Tom was able to raise the $40,000 he needed. Full of gratitude for the outpouring of support, Tom and the Landry's team reflected on the place of gratitude and the difference it had made for them. "There's no work better than our work in the world," Tom says, reflecting on his new perspective. "There's other good work, but there's no better work. It's a gift before it's a burden." The Landry's team vowed to make gratitude a cornerstone of their work.

The immediate crisis averted, Tom turned his attention to preparing the sales force for a strong season the next year. He decided to receive his co-workers at Landry's as gifts and began to encourage others to do the same. He stressed the importance of regarding one another as mystery, maintaining a sense of wonder toward one another. In a fast-paced business setting in which it's easy to view other people merely as objects useful to furthering one's goals, Tom sought to maintain a sense of awe toward each person as a unique human being.

Receiving one another as gift is fundamental to Meg Clapp's servant leadership style and her emphasis on dignity and respect, and it forms the bedrock of the MGH pharmacy department. Beginning with the hiring process, employees are received as gifts. "We hire the best, brightest, and most positive people with the expectation that they will learn, grow, and share the spirit and energy with others." New hires experience their uniqueness from the outset: "We treat each person with the interest and awareness you would expect to experience when you begin a significant relationship."

Meg works hard to cultivate a workplace for people to grow, with an eye toward long-term employment and professional success. She follows up the hiring with a year-long training program, aiming to give people the level of confidence they need to quickly become productive. Each new employee gets a training buddy and receives mentoring throughout the program. Each employee also receives coaching: "We learned long ago that there are all different styles and paces of learning, and therefore we're obligated to coach employees for success." Within a year of hiring, each employee articulates three goals, then receives coaching to achieve those goals, and the management team then commits to helping the person achieve them. Meg seeks to provide an environment that brings out the best in the pharmacists and support staff in her department. Respect for others, fair treatment, caring and concern, listening responsively, and regularly recognizing others' contributions are hallmarks of Meg's practice of receiving her employees as gifts.

Receiving work and one another as gift also forms the backbone of Tom Grant's leadership style. When asked about his leadership at LabOne, Tom betrays his inclination immediately.: "We were so fortunate that we had such great people." Tom naturally recognizes people's gifts, commenting on the strong people skills possessed by some and the strong technical skills possessed by others, and the teams he carefully created showcased that diversity of gifts. While he clearly values business acumen and has been extremely successful financially, Tom focuses first and foremost on personal relationships, regarding his people as the company's strongest assets.

Valuing every employee is core to Tom's way of being, which dictated that he take the time to get to know as many co-workers' names as possible, even when LabOne grew to three thousand employees. Employees at all levels commented on how comfortable they felt with him, how Tom valued them, and how approachable Tom was. Troy Hartman, executive vice-president of sales and marketing at LabOne when Tom was CEO, remarked:

> He is a people person from when he gets up in the morning till the time he goes to bed. He believes in the good in everyone and that everyone has a role to play and can contribute. He comes to people with a natural optimism about the human spirit.

Receiving work and one another as gift rubbed off on others at LabOne. Just as Tom perceived people's gifts before he saw their shortcomings, so also did his leadership team. They learned to strengthen their team by observing how their gifts complemented one another. They learned to value those who reported to them by focusing first on their gifts. They even considered their work overall to be a gift. As Troy Hartman commented:

The thing that was most important to me, having come from other companies, was to come and help establish and be part of the culture that was the gold standard. If you have that direction set from the top that this is how it's going to be, that this is how we're going to treat people and how we expect to be treated, then it permeates the company.

Pioneering Practices of Gratitude

Tom Grant pioneered practices of gratitude at LabOne. Aware that much of the work done by frontline workers opening lab specimens was repetitive and tedious, for example, Tom looked for ways to recognize careful, accurate, efficient work. "One of the biggest mistakes you can make, I think, is to give only a global award based on company earnings. That's hard for the person opening a specimen to relate to." Tom worked with the chief operating officer and others to pioneer practices providing more immediate rewards to frontline employees. They instituted monthly awards (including bonuses) based on how efficiently or how accurately an employee processed a specimen. Employees felt recognized and valued. Those who most needed it received additional compensation directly related to their performance. While the company continued to give global awards, its specific expressions of gratitude to frontline employees enlarged the circle of recognition.

Frustrated in her formative years as she watched managers treat employees dismissively, Meg Clapp vowed to lead differently. As she worked her way up through different leadership roles at the MGH pharmacy, receiving her co-workers as gifts, she began to envision her job as a means of bringing out the best in others. A class at her church, "Unwrapping Your Gifts," helped her understand that her ministry, rather than being something she did at church, lay in her leadership role at work: "Treating people not as hourly workers but as human beings that care as much about patients and MGH as I do — that *is* my ministry."

As part of bringing out the best in everyone, Meg asked her managers and employees what would help them be their best. "We don't feel appreciated," commented a number of employees and managers in the department. "Notice our work and appreciate us." In the perfectionistic culture of a large research hospital, expressions of gratitude weren't the norm. Only inadequate performance was pointed out; excellent performance was taken for granted. In an effort to shift the culture of the department, Meg supported a gratitude initiative by, among other things, purchasing a program called "The Customer" to help train managers and employees in the practice of expressing gratitude.[1] Meg began to pioneer practices of gratitude. The gratitude initiative, involving all managers and staff, focused on "catching people doing things right." Meg herself sought to notice managers' and employees' contributions regularly, and to offer specific appreciation in the moment for work done well. She noticed people lighting up when appreciated, and those around them improved their performance. Managers and staff also began to catch one another doing things right. Pioneering practices of gratitude began to improve the atmosphere in the department.

In order to receive his work as gift and to bring hope to Landry's in a time of uncertainty, Tom Henry began to practice gratitude himself and then invited others to do the same. He pioneered practices of gratitude within the company. For example, to start meetings, inspired by his background in theater, he led "warm-ups," asking the group, "How can you receive your work today as gift, with open heart, with open hands? If our work is a gift, how is it a gift?" The group would then list the ways in which their work that day was gift, rehearsing those things for which they were grateful. "I kept beating that drum, singing that song, meeting after meeting," says Tom.

With steadfast determination, Tom infused the practice of gratitude into the company culture at Landry's.

Creating a Culture of Gratitude

Once he began to introduce gratitude into the workplace, Tom Henry realized what a powerful fuel for energy, creativity, and engagement gratitude could be. He committed himself to transforming Landry's culture in order to create a culture of gratitude. He knew that expressing appreciation from the top has a powerful effect on an organization, but Tom also wanted to encourage co-workers to initiate expressions of gratitude from wherever they stood. He wondered how a culture of gratitude could be fostered throughout the organization, so that thanking one another could become the company's modus operandi, not just an occasional practice, and the power of gratitude could be harnessed for both co-workers' welfare and organizational impact.

Tom began to incorporate gratitude training into new employee orientation. In the first training session he offers new employees, Tom now teaches gratitude first. Tom stresses the importance of thanking team members for every little thing, even things one doesn't want. For example, "If a co-worker comes to tell you there's a phone call from a customer you don't want to talk to, simply say, 'Thank you.' That person took time away from his task to let you know about the phone call. Don't take your frustration out on him." Tom teaches new hires that "you hear a lot of thank yous when you stand in the store" when things go well at Landry's. When Tom stands in the store and doesn't hear those thank-yous, "My radar goes up. It's a symptom of disease in the body." Tom has discovered that when the thank-yous in the store go down, the sales revenues go down, and the customer complaints go up.

At a company retreat, Tom suggested devoting the lunch hour to giving thanks to one another. Employees took turns thanking the person to their left at the table, speaking about one another's gifts, and devoting their attention to appreciating one another. They found that the energy generated by this thanksgiving powerfully fueled their visioning of what the company could be in the year ahead. Now, giving thanks to one another forms one of the cornerstones of the annual company retreat.

Tom also suggested incorporating gratitude into the company's annual review process. Annual reviews now occur among small groups of five to six people meeting together offsite, building the review on a foundation of gratitude. The meeting begins with everyone expressing gratitude for something about the team or a teammate. By beginning with authentic gratitude, hearts are opened and egos are put aside. As a result, the year-end review is characterized by a high degree of honesty. In marked contrast to employees in other companies, Landry's employees say that they can't wait for the next year's review.

At Landry's Bicycles, a culture of gratitude permeates the company, and Tom views gratitude as the foundation of the company's strong esprit de corps. Landry's has found that building a culture on gratitude humanizes the workplace. Paradoxically, seeing other employees as gifts rather than as objects to be used ultimately increases productivity. Business improves, and financial performance increases. Landry's has discovered a well-kept business secret: the power of thanksgiving for employee engagement and business productivity.

AFTER PIONEERING PRACTICES OF GRATITUDE through the gratitude initiative, Meg Clapp sought ways to make gratitude part of the culture of the MGH pharmacy. As part of a larger institution, the pharmacy department faced a challenge Tom Henry didn't have to face. The hospital's perfectionistic culture, noted above, continued to influence the culture of the department. Managers and employees easily slipped back into the attitude of taking one another for granted. Within the department, maintaining a culture of gratitude could be an uphill battle. "It's something we need to continually work on. We don't always do well at it," confesses Meg. Each month she hosts a "bistro lunch" in her office for six employees for the sole purpose of sharing a meal at the table and listening to one another. By returning to the practices of the gratitude initiative, emphasizing dignity and respect, and having regular celebrations within the department, Meg seeks to create and sustain a culture of gratitude.

The department's gratitude initiative has to be brought up periodically and reinforced regularly. From time to time, and especially during times when extra demands are placed on people, Meg or someone else on the leadership team notices that staff members feel overlooked. Ironically, it is during these times, when her team most needs appreciation expressed, that they are most likely to be overlooked, since Meg and the leadership team are also going full bore at those times. When workloads increase, it requires extra effort to see one another as human beings and express appreciation, and the department sometimes succeeds at the effort and sometimes fails.

As part of its effort to create and maintain a culture of gratitude, the department is currently emphasizing dignity and respect in all of their dealings with one another. In a research hospital, where the pecking order is firmly established, those at the lower reaches of the hierarchy typically receive little respect. Even in the higher reaches, dominance is demonstrated by disregarding those one notch lower. Meg seeks to create an oasis of dignity and respect for all in the pharmacy department. By emphasizing an attitude of dignity and respect in one-to-one interactions, meetings, and all communications, Meg hopes that the culture shift in the pharmacy department will eventually have a ripple effect into other parts of the hospital as well.

Celebrations constitute the third element of creating a culture of gratitude at the MGH pharmacy. Meg seeks out opportunities for spontaneous celebration in addition to supporting more formal celebrations. For example, the department recently achieved 93 percent of a goal it had been aiming for, and Meg suggested a spontaneous ice cream celebration to thank everyone who had participated.

Consistently cultivating gratitude, dignity, and respect in the MGH environment is no easy task. How does Meg do it? "Prayer is part of my day and is often the retreat I seek when the work is particularly difficult," she explains. "I offer a 'moment away' to anyone working with me on a difficult situation to take the time to focus on what it is that we're supposed to accomplish. The other person may or may not pray, but I need to make space for the Holy Spirit to be present to the moment." She sees her work as God's work in the world: "Together, we are doing the work of God's love."

What are the results of creating a culture of gratitude? Recently Meg used a spiritual leadership survey to complement her work on dignity and respect among staff, with an eye toward assessing the ethical and spiritual well being of the management team. She was delighted to learn that organizational commitment ranked high among her leadership colleagues, with statements like "I feel my organization appreciates me and my work" and "I would be very happy to spend the rest of my career with this organization" receiving consistently high ratings.

At her last annual review, Meg received the highest grade for human resource management. The MGH pharmacy has become known for its high standards, and its pharmacists are well respected in the medical community. With low turnover and high morale, the department is known as a great place to work. Newcomers, upon first entering the department, often comment that the positive energy is palpable in the reception area. That intuitive sense is borne out in the department's low rate of absenteeism. With its satisfied employees, the department is full of bright, competent professionals who regularly extend themselves for patients.

Through her work at the MGH pharmacy, Meg Clapp has demonstrated that a culture of gratitude, even when sustained in fits and starts, will have a positive effect on the patient and the hospital as a whole. In the midst of a large formal bureaucracy, the pharmacy department shines as a beacon of hope.

AFTER PIONEERING PRACTICES OF GRATITUDE at LabOne, Tom Grant worked consistently to weave those practices into the culture. First and foremost, he cultivated an atmosphere of respect and recognizing the value of every employee:

> It doesn't make any difference who it is in a company, whether you're closing the shop down at night and you're locking up the place or you're cleaning the facility — everybody in a company has an important job to do. I think that it's incredibly important in an organization that everyone recognizes the value of every associate, especially those who aren't making the big dollars.

With this rock-bottom respect as the foundation of the company, a culture of gratitude grew easily.

Tom sowed seeds of gratitude throughout the company. For example, he expressed appreciation by giving generously to employees. In addition to the regular awards given to frontline employees noted above, the company gave generous bonuses to reward superior work at the management level. At seasonal celebrations Tom expressed gratitude to employees by offering generous gifts such as a week at his vacation home in the Cayman Islands, or a week in the company's New York City apartment.

The company's employees, from senior leadership to frontline workers, felt respected and valued in the atmosphere Tom created. Troy Hartman recalls, "We had a very special relationship, no question about it (which I'm confident I'll never have again with a boss or supervisor)."

This culture of gratitude spilled over into giving back to others. Seeing their work as gift, grateful for all they had, employees wanted to give to others. The HR department sponsored opportunities for giving to charities each month, focusing on eyeglasses one month, winter coats another month, and Hurricane Katrina relief or animal shelters in other months. The response from employees, many of whom themselves had relatively little, was phenomenal. Tom Grant had earlier coined the phrase, "The power of One," referring both to the power of the individual and the collective power of LabOne as a company to achieve its mission. Now the phrase caught on as "the power of One" to make a difference in the community and the world, by giving back to others.

Because of the positive atmosphere that resulted from valuing one another and recognizing one another's gifts, recruiting new employees became easy. Employees referred their friends and relatives to LabOne, and whenever a job opening was advertised, qualified applicants flocked to the company. Clients, too, left LabOne after a visit wanting to work there. In Troy Hartman's experience: "Many times I've walked a client out of the building and the person has said, 'What a great culture you have here. Do you have any job openings?'"

Toward the end of Tom Grant's tenure as CEO of LabOne, the HR department submitted an application to the Top 100 Places to work. Although it was unheard of for the contest, LabOne made the first cut in the first year of application. The second year it applied, the company also made the first cut. While the company was acquired the next year before it had a chance to make it to the Top 100, many were convinced that the odds of success were looking good.

Conclusion

Staying on track, in addition to keeping mission at the fore, requires practicing gratitude. The soul wears down under the stress and strain of leadership, and gratitude provides an antidote to this wear and tear. Tom Henry, Meg Clapp, and Tom Grant all know the power of gratitude to strengthen the soul, and they practice it, with varying degrees of success at different times. They receive their work and colleagues as gift, pioneer practices of gratitude in their organizations, and create cultures of gratitude. By practicing gratitude, their souls and the souls of the people they lead are refreshed, their organizations flourish, and their clients are well served.

Queries

1. How have you received your work and colleagues as gift?
2. How have you pioneered practices of gratitude?
3. How have you created cultures of gratitude?

Chapter Six

BATTLING FOR THE SOUL

I N THE MID-1990s, when he was working as director of human resources at CoreStates Bank in Philadelphia, Gus Tolson and the company's CEO faced a rough challenge: how could they stay true to their souls during a merger? The decision to do the merger had already been made: Gus and the CEO were charged with carrying it out. Knowing that the merger would cause a thousand people to lose their jobs, they wondered whether taking part in the process might lead to the erosion of their own values and souls. And what about the souls of those who had to be laid off?

Staying on track involves more than keeping mission at the fore and practicing gratitude, two outward tasks that a leader can perform and encourage others to perform. It also includes something less tangible: battling for the soul. When things aren't going well, the temptation to allow the soul to erode is strong. Staying on track means leading with soul through abundance and lean times alike. How can a leader lead with soul through layoffs, through economic downturns, through mergers?

Furthermore, the temptation to allow the soul to erode can be just as strong in times of abundance. How can leaders battle for the soul when abundance and creature comforts lure them into complacency?

Battling for the soul means keeping soul foremost. It is about caring for the soul — both the leader's own soul and the souls of those the leader leads. How do leaders hold onto their souls, through good times and bad, day in and day out, year after year? Leaders need to battle for their own souls and for the souls of their organizations as they seek to stay on track. How can they achieve this?

Three principles are key: keeping people first, committing to ongoing development, and staying true to values. This chapter will explore each of these principles in turn, illustrating it with examples from the lives of leaders who lived it: Gus Tolson, a human resource professional who has worked in a number of different settings; Tom Hefferon, chairman of Document Management Group in Dublin; and Jean Quinn, founder and co-CEO of Sophia Housing in Dublin.

Keeping People First

The health of the leader's soul and the souls of the people the leader serves depend upon how leaders treat people, both themselves and employees. Battling for the soul involves keeping people first.

THROUGHOUT HIS TWENTY-FIVE-YEAR CAREER as a human resources professional, Gus Tolson has persevered in putting people first. From his varied experiences working in the financial sector, for IBM, in the pharmaceutical industry, and currently for a specialty materials company, Gus has become all too familiar with the forces that exert themselves to push people to second, third, or even last place in an organization. In all his positions, Gus has insisted on considering not only the business impact of every decision, but also the decision's impact on people. Furthermore, he insists that the company communicate with people in a way that maintains their decency and integrity.

Gus commits himself to being the same person at work that he is at home — to bringing his fun-loving, spiritually grounded self to work. Even (perhaps especially) when his company faces major business challenges, Gus draws on all of who he is in order to put people first in the midst of challenging situations.

At CoreStates Bank in the mid-1990s, when facing the merger described at the beginning of this chapter, Gus worked with the company's CEO to design CoreSearch, an internal training program for people in transition. Employees were informed early on about the merger and downsizing, and through CoreSearch, they were offered six months of training while still on salary in order to help place them in new positions.

I n h i s v a r i e d r o l e s leading the company, Tom Hefferon, chairman of the Document Management Group in Dublin, has worked hard to keep people first. As the company has gone through much growth and change in the past thirty years, Tom has found that it's not always easy to keep people first as the forces of entropy and overly simplistic bottom-line thinking exert themselves.

First and foremost, Tom has committed himself and the company to a core respect for people, whether employees or customers. For example, as the company worked to articulate its values, Tom invited employees to gather and list their own personal values. They then identified the values they felt they needed to bring to work with them in order to be whole people, without which they would feel as if they had parked these fundamental values at the door, becoming less than their full selves. As a result, the company values, derived from the employees' list, reflected the personal values of the employees.[1] By gathering values in this way, Tom hoped to help employees derive meaning and significance from their work. Tom has found that tapping into the core of people, respecting their values, and providing a venue for those values to be expressed, allows employees' energy and creativity to be unleashed. "That's what sets the world on fire," he notes.

Once the company's values were articulated, Tom continued his battle to keep people first by putting the values into practice throughout the company. Practices such as taking the time in hiring to carefully assess whether employee and company are a good match, offering truck drivers a four-day work week (with ten-hour days), and giving employees their birthdays off demonstrate how Tom has made it his policy to put people first. In a particularly challenging battle over maternity leave, Tom responded to the argument that the company couldn't afford to let women managers take maternity leave by arguing that maternity leave doesn't happen very often. Furthermore, he argued, women who had achieved the rank of manager often had to be superior to their male counterparts in order to make it to that level, and they were worth every penny that would be invested in them for a maternity leave.

In her challenging work finding homes for homeless people, Jean Quinn, co-CEO of Ireland's Sophia Housing, puts people first. Jean, a Sister of the Daughters of Wisdom community, insists on seeing the image of God (Wisdom) in each person she encounters, even in the messiness of life on the streets. Many in the caring professions can be afflicted by compassion fatigue, an occupational hazard further magnified in those working with the homeless, which leads them to give up on compassionate encounters with the homeless people they serve. The numerous and intricate logistical steps required to house a homeless person can, in themselves, overwhelm a worker, and often it seems like all one can do to simply jump through the hoops of getting the person into a home. Jean knows that keeping her own soul intact means battling for the souls of those she serves, meeting each one as God's unique creation.

Furthermore, Jean battles for the souls of her staff so they can better serve their clients. She puts people first organizationally at

Sophia Housing and treats each employee with respect. Authentic relationships form the core of the community at Sophia.

Committing to Ongoing Development

In the battle for the soul, along with putting people first goes committing to ongoing development, both for the leader and for employees. Both the soul of the leader and the soul of the organization can be eroded when ongoing development is neglected.

AT SOPHIA HOUSING JEAN QUINN commits to her own ongoing development and that of her employees and her clients. First and foremost, she cares for her own soul. Jean learned early on in her work with the homeless how easily one could feel defeated, how easy it was for the work to sap her soul's strength:

> I've been in quite fearful situations. I've known that I needed to talk about this because I was actually very frightened; I was terrified of the people. I felt nauseous inside myself; I didn't much like the people. So I thought, "Well, I'm not suitable to this work." This is going back many, many years now.

Only when she began receiving formal supervision with someone trained in working with the issues she had encountered in people on the street did Jean realize that her feelings were normal. She also sought training in addiction studies and learned to understand what people dealing with addiction needed and how she could help them.

To this day, Jean goes for supervision every two weeks. In choosing a supervisor for herself in her current role, she sought someone outside of the organization, someone with a deep spiritual life, with both psychological training and a background in organizations. She finds that supervision gives her "a sense of safety and confidentiality in exploring my own issues outside of the organization." Working on her own issues that surface at work helps her to be more present to her staff and to her clients and helps her to work more effectively. She also finds that supervision gives her perspective on her work:

> I needed to be away from this place, to begin to see the forest and not simply the trees. That was important for me; it was an appointment I had to keep for myself, and I would honor it. I needed that space if I was to come back to this organization and be able to work in it.

Furthermore, Jean commits to ongoing development for her staff. Knowing how easily people working with the homeless population burn out, she battles for her staff's souls by providing them with ongoing supervision. She offers her staff the opportunity to step back from the chaotic atmosphere of working with the homeless and ask, "What is happening for me in this journey?" For example, Jean noted at a staff meeting how a staff person working with a client who attempted suicide dedicated herself to meeting all the needs of the client, taking her to the hospital, getting her the drugs and psychiatric help she needed, and ensuring that she had a place to go upon release. Then Jean asked what happened to the staff person who was working with the suicidal woman. She makes sure that someone always checks in with her staff: "What happens to staff when they're watching this? You either make a phone call or there's somebody on the spot to ask, 'What happened to you? What's going on for you in this process?' And then follow it up with formal supervision."

A T DOCUMENT MANAGEMENT GROUP, Tom Hefferon also commits to his own and his employees' ongoing development. First and foremost, he cares for his own soul. He spends time each morning in prayer and reflection, and recites short prayers throughout the day, maintaining a running discussion with God. He also maintains a stance of gratitude, recognizing everything he achieves in his work and life as a gift. Tom's local Catholic parish grounds him in spiritual community: "I get my sense of being, my sense of my worth, from

my parish, the way a plant draws from its roots." Tom has participated in many ministries in his parish over the years and feels filled
and nurtured by his participation. In addition, he finds that, in the
midst of his busy life, he can benefit from the more structured spiritual work of retreats and spiritual direction. As a result of his spiritual
practices, Tom says, "I think it makes it a bit easier to stick with a difficult situation, particularly on the people side. I believe that there's
no such thing as a bad person; there's only bad behavior. My belief in
the reality of 'God-in-the-world' gives me perspective."

Document Management Group believes that treating employees
well results in employees who, in turn, treat customers well, and
Tom also commits to ongoing development for his employees. For
example, DMG's "Excellence through People" initiative focused on
providing employees with the skills they needed to be their best selves
at work, while at the same time promising them that management
would treat them with dignity and respect and would communicate
expectations clearly. DMG also offers managers ongoing coaching to
help them strengthen their people skills. Tom believes that "giving is
the best form of receiving," and that as he and senior management
practice this principle, middle managers and frontline employees will
do the same.

Gus Tolson commits to ongoing development for himself and
for his employees. First and foremost for Gus is care of his own soul.
He finds strength for carrying out his demanding job in his Christian
faith: "My source of strength is twofold: It is the Lord, and it is the
best book around, the Bible."

Outside of work, Tolson regrounds himself in God in order to
return to work with fresh perspective. He finds that spending time
reading the Bible refreshes his soul and regrounds him in his values. Drawing on the wisdom of his mentor at church also helps him
reconnect with God and link his faith to his challenges at work.

Gus respects the policies of his current company toward religion, which include encouraging the formation of network groups based on gender or ethnicity, but not on religion. In keeping with this approach, he elects not to bring his Bible to the office, nor does he talk explicitly about his faith at work. At the same time, he finds that work goes better when he is fully himself, and being fully himself includes practicing his faith in ways appropriate to his workplace. When he needs grounding at work, Tolson shuts his office door and prays. When he's facing a challenging meeting or a difficult employee situation, a break for prayer provides the wisdom and compassion he needs. "Sometimes in meetings," says Gus, "I've had to shut my eyes and call on the Lord to get me through something." He finds that prayer often shifts his perspective and reveals a way forward he hadn't seen before.

In addition to prayer, Gus has discovered that connecting with spiritual people at work helps him to stay grounded. "Although we may not talk about the Lord in the workplace, because we are aligned philosophically, spiritually, and so forth, just going and having lunch with that person makes the connection and gives me the kind of energy I need." While Gus and his colleagues don't talk about their faith at work, they sense an underlying commonality. They discover that they are kindred spirits, and they turn to one another for support when the road gets rough.

Gus has learned that he doesn't need to check his faith at the door. Finding appropriate ways to draw on prayer and connect with spiritual people at work helps him to bring his full self to work and, as a result, to better serve the company.

Gus Tolson also commits to ongoing development of employees. For example, in a move that was highly unusual at the time, the CoreSearch training program he helped to design committed to the ongoing development of employees in transition. For six months, employees came to work every day and worked on developing new skills.

They received training and worked temporarily in other parts of the business to gain expertise in new areas.

In designing CoreSearch, Gus consulted with external search firms to understand the psyche of a person in transition — a person who's been told that his job is ending, that he must find a new job with the company's help. The company wanted to create an environment in which people could feel good about themselves in the midst of their transitions. The process was designed around the person's needs rather than those of the company. "It would have been really easy for us to take the shortcut and not really think about the person, the individual, but just the organization," Gus says. But the company didn't take the shortcut. Based on what he had learned, Gus provided everyone with office space and told them, "You're still going to have a place that you can call your own. We want you to put pictures up there and make it yours. You're still going to get a paycheck. You're going to continue to report to work."

In the end, the program boasted a placement rate of 84 percent and cost the company a few million dollars. Many employees expressed grateful sentiments: "I appreciate the effort that you demonstrated, the commitment that you made, to trying to keep me whole." Even those employees who didn't get jobs immediately had time for their transition and were treated with dignity and respect. Because of Gus's commitment to developing people, shared by the company's CEO, a merger that could have spelled tragedy for many people became an opportunity to learn new skills and to move forward into fulfilling work.

Staying True to Values

The health of both the leader's and the organization's souls depends upon staying true to their values. Gus Tolson has battled for his own soul and the souls of the companies he has served by continuing to stand up for his own values and the values his companies espouse.

When seeking employment, Gus looks for companies whose values align with his own values. In his twenty-five years in human resources, Gus has sought to work for companies that are committed to sustainability, to strengthening the communities they inhabit, to integrity, to diversity, and, as noted above, to putting people first.

Staying true to values, day in and day out, is no easy task. For example, in the area of diversity, Gus faces constant challenges. Gus likens the workforce of a company to an orchestra, which requires the full complement of instruments in order to produce the best music. In his current role as director of North America staffing for the Rohm and Haas company, Gus sees himself as a conductor assembling his orchestra. With the goal of recruiting a diverse workforce, Gus challenges his team to find strong minority candidates. But with respect to engineers, Gus hears the constant refrain, "We just can't find minority engineers. They're just not out there." Gus finds himself in the position of standard bearer, constantly bringing the company back to its core value of diversity. Although African Americans and Hispanics currently constitute only 3 percent of North American Ph.D.s in chemistry, Gus maintains that pointing at the low percentage provides an easy way out of pursuing the minority candidates that do exist. When Gus hears a comment about the low numbers:

> I find myself saying, "Okay, you can let that comment go, or you can try to educate." Because, by people saying there aren't that many, they're casting a cloud over the ability to achieve it. And if nothing is said, then potentially you could now have a room of twenty more people who will wipe their hands and say, "Okay, so that's why we shouldn't try to recruit women in engineering, or minorities in chemistry."

Gus can grow weary constantly fighting the battle for recruiting minorities, yet he knows that often he is the only one in the room who understands the issue. He feels that if he doesn't speak up, the opportunity to educate others will pass: "It plays out further in my being a person of color where I'm too often selected as the spokesperson for all the others. I'm speaking as the representative African American, as one of the few in management." Gus consistently raises the question, "What are we doing to recruit the 3 percent? How do we need to change our culture in order to appeal to the minority candidate?" When he grows battle-weary, Gus prays for the strength to persevere, to maintain his integrity in speaking up for what is right.

While assembling a diverse orchestra presents ongoing challenges, bringing out the sounds of the various instruments presents challenges as well. When Gus facilitates a meeting, he commits himself to bringing out all the voices. The diversity of perspectives gained in hiring people of different races, ethnicities, national origins, genders, and educational backgrounds is lost if one perspective dominates a meeting. Gus seeks diversity of thought in meetings. He creates a safe space for everyone and encourages those who are silent to express their points of view.

B ECAUSE HIS COMPANY LOST ITS VALUES for a time, Tom Hefferon knows the importance of staying true to values. In 2005, Tom moved out of his role as managing director of Document Management Group and into the role of chairman. Over the course of the next two years, the company lost its way. Tom attributes the company's floundering to his own inability to see the forest for the trees. As the company struggled, it (1) became dysfunctional in its operations, and (2) slid away from its values. When Tom realized what had happened, he knew that his task was to (1) call the company back to its values and (2) get the company operating smoothly.

What had happened? In 2003 and 2004, DMG had been listed as one of the top five Best Companies to work for in Ireland. Furthermore, in 2003, it had received the additional honor of being named no. 1 in Camaraderie. For the previous fifteen years, its values of respect, creativity, and camaraderie had been instrumental in making the company what it was.[2] But by 2005, DMG, a result of the merging of several business-to-business service companies, needed to make the transition from multiple small entrepreneurial companies to one professionally managed company. Tom and his business partner, cofounders of the companies that made up DMG, knew that the time had come to turn over the company's management to a professional. Together Tom, his business partner, and the board determined that Tom should move to the role of chairman in order to maintain continuity in the big picture of values and mission, while a professional manager would take over the day-to-day operations. Tom and his partner also realized that, like most entrepreneurs, they lacked strategy skills, and deputized the new managing director with strategy responsibilities.

The new managing director, chosen for his abilities to manage professionally and to develop strategy, assured the board that he ascribed to DMG's values. However, over time it became clear that, while he viewed the values as attractive icing on the cake when everything else was going well, he didn't want to be pinned to them when the going got tough. When he found himself in a pinch, he sacrificed those values for other gains, rewriting the values he found too constraining. For example, while in theory he ascribed to DMG's value of including all voices in decision making, in practice he exercised a command-and-control style of leadership. The vibrant, creative atmosphere for which the company had become known slowly deteriorated.

Meanwhile, the company became more and more dysfunctional, and the managing director, to compensate, became more and more controlling. In retrospect Tom realized that he and his partner bore part of the responsibility for not fully letting go, thus perhaps setting up the new managing director for failure. In late 2006, the managing director and the board collided over strategy, and the managing director subsequently left. Meanwhile, DMG had fallen out of the top 10 Best Companies in 2005, and bottomed out of the Top 50 completely in 2006. In fact, a number of employees filling out the questionnaires that made up part of the Best Companies selection process admitted that they no longer liked going to work at DMG.

With much soul-searching, Tom and the other board members began to untangle the threads as they asked themselves, "What went wrong?" Tom and his business partner, realizing they had not fully made the transition from entrepreneurial to professional management mind-set, admitted their mistake to the board and committed themselves to letting go of day-to-day management. Tom also steeped himself in the literature about how entrepreneurial companies make the transition to professional management, identifying, with the help of an organizational psychologist, the places DMG had gone astray and the ways in which the company needed to get back on track. As Tom observes, "Just as an individual can become mentally unstable, so can an organization become behaviorally unstable. That's where we found ourselves."

If psychologically the company had become behaviorally unstable, spiritually it had fallen into sin. "It surprised me how utterly lost we could get," muses Tom. In his battle for the company's soul, he focused on rearticulating its values and, more important, helping the company believe in its soul again. The company's overarching values were rearticulated as "work, worth, and well-being," noting the reciprocity of each one. For instance, "work" means both providing good work for employees and expecting good work from them, while "worth" refers both to an employee's sense of self-worth and to the worth the company asks employees to generate. "Well-being," in turn, denotes an employee's sense of health and well-being as well as the employee's contribution to the company's well-being, economic and otherwise. "Your values are your guiding light. When you're in the maelstrom, they're the only things that *can* guide you," explained Tom in a recent company meeting. Rather than letting go of values when times get tough, Tom exhorted managers to turn to the values as their plumb line.

Ultimately, in the summer of 2007 a division manager who was deeply committed to DMG's values assumed the role of managing director, and the company started its long, slow climb to recovery. Tom and the new managing director, in an effort to put decision making power back into the hands of the employees, instituted a "bottom-up" strategy plan followed by a budgeting process for the year ahead. Instead of higher-ups decreeing what employees are required to accomplish within a predetermined budget, an approach that invites resistance, employees are asked to design a budget that allows them to accomplish their goals. Tom has learned that, often, senior managers need to help employees ramp down their goals, as they overreach when they use the "bottom-up" approach.

DMG's fall and subsequent nascent recovery demonstrates to Tom that, even from the highest pinnacle, a company can still find itself susceptible to temptations and dysfunctionalities. Leaders must vigilantly battle for their own souls and the souls of the organizations they lead.

At Sophia Housing, Jean Quinn knows the importance of staying true to values. Before she founded Sophia, Jean worked for years on the streets, helping homeless people find housing. Six months after finding housing for them, Jean would see the same people back on the streets again, because their core issues hadn't been addressed. Frustrated with this state of affairs, she founded Sophia Housing, committing to a more holistic approach toward homelessness. She wanted to attend to the deepest levels of the people she was serving as well as to their physical needs.

This holistic approach, Sophia's core value, hasn't always been easy to stay true to. For example, Jean committed to providing a Wisdom Centre in a central location of each housing complex that Sophia builds. In Jean's vision, the Wisdom Centre would provide a space for reflection or prayer, a healing place to get away from the fray and nurture the soul. When the architect's plans came back for the first building, the construction of a Wisdom Centre added 1.2 million to the cost. Despite the board's protests about cost, Jean remained unwaveringly faithful to Sophia's core value of nurturing the soul as well as the body. The Wisdom Centre stayed in the plans.

Staying true to the core value of maintaining a holistic approach has helped Jean Quinn battle for the souls of her clients and of her staff and, as a result, has helped her to build a more effective organization. Moreover, the holistic approach has caused her to battle for her own soul:

> My journey started out many, many years ago, in working with people who are out of home. Going into supervision, I discovered I was so out of home myself, realizing that I had issues that were never addressed in my life and discovering a whole world.

The holistic approach has nurtured Jean's deepest self, the deepest selves of her staff, and the deepest selves of Sophia's clients. Of the holistic approach, Jean and the her staff have been surprised to discover, "It's not for the people out there; it's for all of us."

Conclusion

Staying on track, through abundance and lean times alike, isn't easy. Through the temptations that arise at either extreme, leaders face the battle for their own souls and the souls of those they serve. Gus Tolson, Tom Hefferon, and Jean Quinn all kept people first, committed to ongoing development, and stayed true to their values through numerous challenges. They battled for the soul repeatedly and saw their efforts pay off in terms of morale, integrity, and reputation. Battling for the soul, an essential element of staying on track, results in strengthened leaders, deepened souls, and solid organizations.

Queries

1. How have you kept people first in the groups you lead?

2. How have you committed to ongoing development of your soul and the souls of those you lead?

3. How have you stayed true to your values?

PART THREE

PERSEVERING TO THE END

Chapter Seven

BREAKING THE CYCLE OF VIOLENCE

I N December of 1995 after South African apartheid had ended, Archbishop Desmond Tutu was named head of the country's Truth and Reconciliation Commission. South Africa had had to come to terms with how it would bring to justice perpetrators of crimes under the old regime. Retributive justice was not only too costly for the financially strapped country, but would also result in winners and losers and could easily backfire. Blanket amnesty, on the other hand, would leave the victims unacknowledged, in effect victimizing them again. How was the country to move forward? South Africa had achieved independence. How could the country's leaders persevere to the end and bring about a stable government after so much turmoil?

Leaders who choose the path of leading with soul and manage to stay on track must eventually face the question of whether they will persevere to the end. The further the leader goes on the path of soul, the higher the stakes. Persevering to the end requires leaders to understand and embrace the second half of the journey (to be discussed in chapter 8), seek spiritual guidance (to be discussed in chapter 9), and understand and come to terms with violence. A soulful leader must learn to break the cycle of violence.

While violence may seem to be limited to countries at war and ghettos under siege, it actually rears its ugly head in virtually all human institutions, whether nations, families, or organizations. The question for leaders is not *whether* they will encounter violence but *how* they will encounter it. Leaders who want to persevere to the end, leading with soul, to bring about deep and lasting transformation, must eventually face violence and their own response to it. This chapter will examine three aspects of breaking the cycle of violence: seeing compassionately, interrupting the cycle, and forgiving, illustrated by examples from the lives of three leaders who practice them: Desmond Tutu, Archbishop Emeritus of the Anglican Church in South Africa; Genny Nelson, cofounder of Sisters of the Road Café in Portland, Oregon; and Clarena Tolson, streets commissioner for the city of Philadelphia.

Seeing Compassionately

Breaking the cycle of violence begins with seeing compassionately: to break the cycle of violence, one must first see with the eyes of the heart. Through compassion, violence is transformed.

Seeing compassionately for Desmond Tutu grows out of prayer. It was prayer that undergirded his work with the Truth and Reconciliation Commission, just as prayer had undergirded his ministry before that. As the Truth and Reconciliation Commission began to work toward uniting a divided country, Desmond Tutu turned to God for strength and guidance. Only through frequent, regular prayer was Tutu able to regard everyone, both victims and perpetrators, with compassion. "I wouldn't have survived without fairly substantial chunks of quiet and meditation," the archbishop declares emphatically. "The demands that are made on one almost always seem to be beyond one's natural capacities. There would be many times when the problems, the crises we were facing seemed about to overwhelm us. There's no way in which you could have confronted these in your own strength."

In addition to his personal prayer times, Tutu has called on others to pray for him, especially in times of great need:

> It is such a good thing to know at those times that you are part of a wonderful communion, a wonderful body, and there are those who are far more holy than you who are able to worship God with a depth of feeling and fervor which you are not feeling at all, which you are not experiencing. And you are borne on this current of worship and adoration, and all you need to do is throw yourself into the stream and you are carried.... When we started with the Truth and Reconciliation Commission in South Africa, I wrote to the secretary-general of the Anglican consultative council and asked him if he could please put this request to the religious communities of our church around the world, to say, "Please pray for this enterprise."

By establishing the Truth and Reconciliation Commission, South Africa chose a third way, distinct from both retributive justice and blanket amnesty. By inviting perpetrators to apply for amnesty in exchange for full disclosure of their crimes, South Africa chose *restorative* justice. Leaders of the Commission had to learn to see with compassion as they carried out their difficult work. For eighteen months, the Commission heard case after case, listening to victims as well as to perpetrators. Tutu says:

> We in the Commission were quite appalled at the depth of depravity to which human beings could sink.... We had to distinguish between the deed and the perpetrator, between the sinner and the sin, to hate and condemn the sin while being filled with compassion for the sinner.[1]

Tutu found himself stretched to offer compassion to perpetrators on both sides, and his heart grew larger in the process.

GENNY NELSON, COFOUNDER OF SISTERS OF THE ROAD, a café, resource, and community organizing center for homeless people in Portland, Oregon, had to learn to see compassionately from her first day working at the Everett Street Service Center, a Portland homeless shelter. Listening to the stories of the men who came to the shelter, Genny saw them with new eyes and began to view them with compassion.[2] They urged her to stand in their shoes:

> They encouraged us over and over again to try eating at the missions and soup lines, which we did. I think had we not done that, something would have been missing from Sisters. It was very humbling to be in those situations alongside the folks that we knew, members of this community.[3]

As she and Sisters cofounder Sandy Gooch visited mission after soup line after mission, they discovered the pitfalls of overly structured and impersonalized meal services:

> So many of the missions and soup lines were very institutionalized. Folks couldn't talk to one another, and breaking bread with your friends and family is a whole act of building relationship, strengthening the feelings between you, and finding out those new things about what's happening to each other. That kind of magic occurs over a meal. I was really humbled, as was Sandy.[4]

A significant turning point for Genny came one day as she stood alongside the people she had been serving, waiting in a long line for breakfast at a mission on a cold morning. When the group finally got inside and finished listening to the required pre-meal sermon, they were served old, barely recognizable ice cream for breakfast. Then and there, Genny determined to provide a setting in which people could dine with dignity, a place where they could work or pay for hot, nutritious meals.

Genny also learned to see compassionately as she and Sandy Gooch listened to the specific plights of homeless women. Genny learned that these women longed above all for a safe place. As she listened to their stories, Genny heard repeated tales of violence: robbery, beating, and rape. The streets weren't safe. The shelters, which often had only one small section for women (if they had anything for women at all), weren't safe. Even the restrooms weren't safe. Genny and Sandy made a commitment to founding a safe place for homeless people, especially women and children: Sisters of the Road Café.

Furthermore, Genny learned to see compassionately when she supervised Sisters' employees. Since many employees initially walked through the door as customers, they needed to learn what was required of them as employees. At Sisters of the Road, compassion and accountability go together. The café is known as a place where one can make a mistake and still be loved, where one can make a mistake and be called on to be one's best self. In reflecting on how compassion and accountability are integrated in Sisters' staff, Genny states:

> If your behavior is inappropriate, we're not going to pretend ignorance. The supervisor will sit down with the employee and say, "You know what — this behavior can't happen. It's got to change. So talk to me about what you need from Sisters, and I will talk to you about what I need from you, and let's check in in the next week or so."

If the inappropriate behavior persists, Sisters follows a transparent step-by-step process which, on rare occasions, culminates in dismissal. While dismissal is difficult, it's not unusual for a dismissed employee to appreciate the process in retrospect, reflecting:

> Oh man, was I really pissed when you let me go. But I got to thinking about how I was treated; the process works the same for

all staff. I understand the decision now; you told me the truth. Sisters is the best place I've ever worked.

For Genny, seeing compassionately provides the foundation for a new kind of relationship and, ultimately, for breaking the cycle of violence.

FOR CLARENA TOLSON, seeing compassionately grows out of prayer. While Archbishop Desmond Tutu leads with compassion on an international scale and Genny Nelson leads compassionately in the midst of life on the streets, Clarena Tolson has learned to lead with compassion in the nitty-gritty daily life of city government. As streets commissioner for the city of Philadelphia, Clarena prays for a heart of compassion toward the mayor to whom she reports, toward the City Council and her fellow commissioners, toward the nearly two thousand workers in her department for whom she is responsible, and toward everyone with whom she comes into contact. In the midst of the conflicts that crop up in city politics, seeing with compassion provides Clarena with a foundation for transforming the atmosphere.

For Clarena, transforming the workplace atmosphere begins with respect for everyone. She prays that she may view all the workers in her department with respect. In a department that focuses to a large extent on garbage collection, Clarena focuses on pride:

> I instill a sense of pride in our employees about the honor of their jobs and their real role — they don't just take trash, they provide a safe environment for children to go to school and for seniors to navigate our streets. So whether our employees are collecting trash or digging ditches or designing bridges, there's a level of professionalism, there's a level of respect, and there's a responsibility that they have, which is an honor to have.

Seeing compassionately and respectfully serves the department well, especially in the midst of veiled or open conflict, as will be seen below.

Interrupting the Cycle

After learning to see with compassion, a leader must interrupt the cycle of violence in order to ultimately break it. Clarena Tolson has discovered that this principle applies as well to daily life in city government as it does in more obvious venues of conflict and violence. For example, in departmental budget hearings before the city council, political infighting easily erupts. Rather than fighting fire with fire, Clarena seeks to interrupt the cycle of conflict. Referring to challenges in the budget process, Clarena says:

> I pray that others' hearts and minds will be open to hear what they have to hear, and that I will do nothing to offend them, and that their hearts be softened to move toward a resolution of problems, versus engaging in battle for the sake of battle.

She seeks to remain open to what she can learn from their perspective, while also seeking to engage them in constructive dialogue regarding her perspective. How well does this approach work? After all, it could sound like nothing more than a pious thought from someone who isn't "tough enough" to take people on. Yet Clarena often finds her colleagues commenting on how easily she got through the budget hearing process, in contrast to the experiences of those in other departments.

Occasionally Clarena has found herself in the position of interrupting the cycle of more obvious violence. On one occasion, when she was serving as a senior manager in the department before her promotion to commissioner, violence erupted at a worksite some distance from hers, and the then commissioner sent her directly to the scene while he called the police and dealt with other matters. Some employees at the scene were eager to respond with hostility, Clarena found, and others wanted to run away, but Clarena offered a third alternative, calling the group to prayer:

We gathered to pray for those who'd been badly harmed (we didn't know at the moment that they'd been killed) and to pray for the person who did the shooting, pray for his family, for all that they would be going through. And that was a real challenge as I was standing there and the room was bloody, and the bodies were being carried out as we stood there. It was difficult to keep the focus on prayer.

Through her prayers at the scene of the violence, Clarena was able to calm the group and to help them take the first steps toward returning to normalcy. Her prayer interrupted the cycle of violence and prevented it from escalating.

GENNY NELSON INTERRUPTED the cycle of violence toward homeless women in two ways. First, she did so by cofounding Sisters of the Road Café with Sandy Gooch in 1979. Founded on the principles of nonviolence and gentle personalism, Sisters eschews violence of all kinds, and thus has provided a different atmosphere from that which the women had experienced elsewhere.

It wasn't easy to create a new kind of environment. Genny reflects:

I had since 1972 been formally introduced to nonviolence, not only as a philosophy but as a way of life. It was very challenging the first couple of years because there was no other organization on the street that offered their services from a philosophy of nonviolence and gentle personalism.[5]

Second, Genny and all the staff at Sisters of the Road interrupted the cycle of violence by daily practicing the tenets of nonviolence wherever Sisters work took them, in or outside the café. Once Sisters of the Road Café had been established and its philosophy articulated, the rubber met the road. Because Sisters operated from a different premise than other institutions in the neighborhood, Genny needed a concrete definition of nonviolence and the consequences of ignoring it that she could communicate to customers and volunteers. She and Sandy came up with guidelines for intervening whenever physical or verbal violence occurred and began putting them to use. She reflects on how customers responded:

> People can be quiet as a mouse when they first come in and watch how staff interact with customers when conflict occurs. Practicing nonviolence doesn't mean the absence of conflict. It is the commitment to stay present to the conflict, to not dismiss it, and then participate in resolution.

For example, on one occasion a woman walked into the café, followed fifteen minutes later by a man who, suggesting by his demeanor that he owned her, indicated that they had to leave. Knowing she needed to intervene, Genny introduced herself to the man and said:

> You know, you're really welcome to be here, but this woman just sat down and she's eating her meal and she gets to do that in peace. So I'm going to ask you to find another place in the café to sit down, and you can order up whatever you like.[6]

The man moved away grudgingly, and after ordering a cup of coffee, stormed out. Later Genny learned that the woman was a prostitute, the man her pimp. Word spread quickly on the street that Sisters was a place where even prostitutes would be treated with respect and that they would be safe from pimps' harassment inside its doors.

Additionally, Genny helped interrupt the cycle of violence by effecting systemic change. In 2001 she took on the role of director of community organizing and systemic change for Sisters of the Road. Recognizing the lack of a systemic approach to end homelessness, Sisters began addressing this by expanding its community organizing efforts at the beginning of the new millennium. Out of the community organizing work was born Crossroads, a partnership between the homeless and the housed that addressed the violence of homelessness through research and organizing. Genny oversaw the Crossroads research project, which interviewed six hundred homeless people, produced a book in their voice, and published a manual showing how others could carry out a similar project in their locale. In her view, the research and organizing has helped interrupt the cycle of violence against people dealing with homelessness by bearing witness to their truth, and that truth has propelled them into leadership training and direct action with their peers instead of despair and complacency.

ON NUMEROUS OCCASIONS, Desmond Tutu interrupted the cycle of violence in South Africa — during his service on the Truth and Reconciliation Commission and at other times. For example, on September 6, 1989, when apartheid was still in full force, peaceful protests were held in South Africa to boycott a racist election. Aiming indiscriminately, state security forces shot and killed twenty people, including children standing in their own yards. Upon receiving the news, Tutu ran into the chapel of his Capetown archbishop's residence, crying and beseeching God, "How could you let this happen?" It would have been easy to respond in fear, allowing the government to continue its intimidation of the country's blacks or, conversely, to respond with hostility, joining those who called for armed resistance, but Desmond Tutu chose neither. When the archbishop emerged from his prayer, he announced that there would be a peaceful protest march. "It seemed like God was saying that the response was to call for a protest march," he subsequently reflected. The march, held on September 13, drew thirty thousand people, the first in a series of major protests that, in Tutu's words, "marked the beginning of the end for apartheid." In announcing "we won't stand for this violence" while at the same time making the statement peacefully, the protestors were able to interrupt the country's cycle of violence. Less than five months later, on February 2, 1990, Prime Minister de Klerk announced the end of apartheid.

On another occasion, in the midst of the work of the Truth and Reconciliation Commission, Desmond Tutu interrupted the cycle of violence in a different way. In 1997, the Commission was holding hearings regarding violent reprisals toward suspected government collaborators that were allegedly masterminded by Winnie Madikizela-Mandela, President Nelson Mandela's ex-wife. As the evidence mounted, the Commission was forced to the conclusion that Winnie Madikizela-Mandela might very well be guilty of torture and murder. Claiming innocence with a proud demeanor, she didn't ask for forgiveness. While the natural response toward such behavior would be hardheartedness in return for her own hardheartedness or to feel a sense of defeat in the face of her unwillingness to yield, Desmond Tutu chose another way. At the end of the hearing, he turned to her and made an impassioned plea. Beginning with his family's relationship with her, a close relationship over many years, and then affirming her as an icon of liberation, he appealed to her:

> There are people out there who want to embrace you. I still embrace you because I love you and I love you very deeply. There are many out there who would have wanted to do so if you were able to bring yourself to say something went wrong.... Say, "I am sorry; I am sorry for my part in what went wrong." I beg you, I beg you, I beg you please.... You are a great person and you don't know how your greatness would be enhanced if you were to say sorry, things went wrong, forgive me.[7]

Madikizela-Mandela responded, expressing sorrow for her victims' families:

> Thank you very much for your wonderful, wise words.... That is the father I have always known in you.... I am saying it is true, things went horribly wrong. I fully agree with that and for that part of those painful years when things went horribly wrong and we were aware of the fact that there were factors that led to that, for that I am deeply sorry.[8]

While some viewed Winnie Madikizela-Mandela's apology as luke-warm, for her it was a major step. The archbishop reflected:

> I am not sure that we are right to scoff at even what might appear a halfhearted request for forgiveness. It is never easy to say, "I am sorry"; they are the hardest words to articulate in any language. I often find it difficult to say them even in the intimacy of my bedroom to my wife. We can imagine how much more difficult it must be to utter them in the full glare of TV lights and media publicity.
>
> The prophet Isaiah speaks of the servant of God who is gentle and does not blow out a flickering flame. I think this was the very first time Mrs. Madikizela-Mandela had apologized in public, and that was something for someone as proud as she.[9]

Archbishop Tutu had interrupted the cycle of violence on another occasion, when security forces killed thirty-eight people in Sebokeng, a black township, in 1990. Word of the massacre came to him while in the midst of a meeting with his synod of bishops at a conference center in Lesotho. He left the meeting to cry and pray in the chapel and then, feeling directed by God, returned to the bishops. Reflecting on the event later, he recounted urging the bishops to:

> . . . suspend our meeting, which had never happened before, and go [to Sebokeng]. And the bishops, all of them, unanimously agreed. We put aside our whole agenda, and went.

The bishops left Lesotho for Sebokeng early the next morning, celebrated the Eucharist in a local church when they arrived, and then toured Sebokeng, visiting the injured and the bereaved. While the bishops were speaking with a crowd of young people gathered in the streets, a convoy of Casspirs (armored police vehicles with teargas and machine guns) appeared. John Cleary of the Australian Broadcasting Corporation reported what he observed:

I heard the archbishop say, "Let us pray." Then the noise of the vehicles stopped. The crowd went quiet. There was no sound from the Casspirs, no sound of teargas canisters. So I looked around and there, behind me, were the Anglican bishops of Southern Aftrica — black, white, coloured, old, young — standing between the crowd and the Casspirs, with their arms outstretched. In that moment, I understood a little about what the Christian vision for a new South Africa cost people. I'd never witnessed that sort of courage before.[10]

The bishops of Southern Africa succeeded in interrupting the cycle of violence before it escalated even further in Sebokeng township.

On another occasion, Desmond Tutu sought to interrupt the cycle of violence with the former president of South Africa. P. W. Botha, South Africa's prime minister from 1978 to 1984, during the height of apartheid, and then president from 1984 to 1989, was consistently implicated in the Truth and Reconciliation Commission hearings. Although the Commission possessed the right to subpoena anyone for a hearing, even a former president, Tutu himself arranged a visit with Botha, hoping that a face-to-face meeting would encourage the ex-president to cooperate. Despite the extensive suffering he and his people had endured under Botha's leadership and despite Botha's reputation for stubbornness, Desmond Tutu prayed that he would encounter the ex-president with an open heart. Tutu traveled a considerable distance to see Botha, and they met for tea at Botha's daughter's residence. Responding to Tutu's appeal, Botha agreed to cooperate with the Commission but insisted upon answering their questions in writing (he refused to come to a hearing in person), with an additional provision that the new government furnish him with access to government documents and money for his legal fees. President Mandela agreed to go the extra mile and pay Botha's legal fees and give him access to government documents, but Botha still dragged his feet in responding to the Commission's questions.

By the time Botha had submitted his written response to the Commission's questions, new evidence had surfaced, and the Commission was asking Botha, along with other officials of the former government, to appear before them in person. Botha refused, and the Commission sent him a subpoena. When he ignored the subpoena, he was arraigned by the attorney general of his region for refusing to respond to it. Some who had suffered under Botha were delighted that their former oppressor would at last be on trial, experiencing the retributive justice that he deserved. Nevertheless, the Commission continued to reach out to the ex-president, even offering to meet him near his home so that he could obey the subpoena and avoid a court trial. Again, Botha refused. Serving as a witness at Botha's court trial, Desmond Tutu made one last attempt from the witness stand. Addressing the judge, he pled:

> Your worship, I believe that we still have an opportunity — although this is a court of law, and without suggesting that the accused is guilty of any violations, I speak on behalf of people who have suffered grievously as a result of policies that were carried out by governments, including the government that [Botha] headed. I want to appeal to him. I want to appeal to him to take this chance... to say that he may not himself even [have] intended the suffering.... He may not have given orders or authorized anything.... I am just saying that the government that he headed caused many of our people deep, deep anguish and pain and suffering. Our people want to be part of this country and to be part of reconciliation.
>
> If Mr. Botha was able to say: I am sorry that the policies of my government caused you pain. Just that. Can he bring himself to say I am sorry that the policies of my government caused you so much pain? That would be a tremendous thing, and I appeal to him.[11]

Botha responded only in anger, defiant to the end. The trial resumed, and Botha was convicted.

Was Tutu's effort to interrupt the cycle of violence, to plead for reconciliation rather than retributive justice, wasted in this case? Who can say? In reaching out to Botha, Desmond Tutu did everything humanly possible to offer a third way, a new way forward, for the people of South Africa. Although Botha didn't respond, Tutu could at least know that in offering the olive branch he had left no stone unturned. Furthermore, the seeds sown through this public act of reaching out may have penetrated other hearts more open than Botha's, hearts that allowed the seeds to grow and mature, bearing fruit in their season. Words of compassion and invitation are rarely wasted.

Forgiving

Breaking the cycle of violence also includes forgiving. Once the cycle of violence is interrupted through openhearted invitation and apology, the circle of transformation is completed by forgiveness.

Forgiveness formed the backbone of South Africa's Truth and Reconciliation Commission. As leader of the Commission, unflinchingly facing the truth of the horrors propagated by and on South Africa's people, Desmond Tutu also prayed to forgive.

The Commission was committed to reconciliation in South Africa through forgiveness. It was structured to facilitate forgiveness by (1) setting a fixed term of two years for its operation, (2) collecting statements, and (3) holding public hearings. The two-year fixed term was chosen so that those who desired amnesty would have ample time to apply for it and so that the process would have a clear ending, with no unfinished business left for the new government. The Commission organized trained people to collect statements throughout the country, collecting twenty thousand victims' statements in all, more than had ever been collected in similar processes elsewhere. Public hearings were set up in districts across the country, urban and rural, in such venues as town halls, civic centers, and churches. Due to the mammoth outpouring of response to the call for victims' statements, only about one victim in ten received a public hearing. Those who did not receive a public hearing were assured by the Commission that their written statements would be taken just as seriously as the statements of those who testified publicly.

The Commission heard victims from both sides, both victims of the white apartheid government and victims of rebel forces. Tutu found himself inspired to forgive by the victims who forgave:

> Mercifully and wonderfully, as I listened to these stories of victims I marveled at their magnanimity, that after so much suffering, instead of lusting for revenge, they had this extraordinary willingness to forgive.[12]

The Commission also opened itself to applications for amnesty from perpetrators on both sides. Many exhibited courage, providing full disclosure of their misdeeds. Brian Mitchell, a police captain, asked for forgiveness from a devastated rural community where his orders had resulted in the killing of eleven innocent people, mostly women and children. He asked the Commission to arrange for him to visit the community and expressed his desire to be involved in its reconstruction. Desmond Tutu related Mitchell's visit to the community:

> It could have gone badly wrong. It was a difficult and tense meeting at the beginning, with everybody a little awkward and the community understandably hostile.... The atmosphere began to change, to ease, after a while. While one or two of the victims were still not too keen to forgive him, the majority were glad he had come, and by the time he left things had improved so much that they were waving him goodbye quite warmly.[13]

Through forgiveness, the Truth and Reconciliation Commission saw, again and again, how the cycle of violence could be broken and the circle of transformation completed.

FORGIVENESS FORMS THE FOUNDATION of Genny Nelson's leadership at Sisters of the Road. She reflects: "I don't think you can practice nonviolence without forgiveness. It is forgiveness of people who have harmed you and equally their forgiveness when you have harmed them—and ultimately forgiveness of one's self."

For example, whenever a staff member utilizes nonviolent means to interrupt a verbal or physical conflict at the café, participants in the conflict are expected to cease and desist and are invited to reconcile with one another. Often Genny and other staff members must practice forgiveness as they become the targets of the violence they interrupt, and they must both ask for forgiveness and forgive themselves when they do not respond as fairly or compassionately as needed. The staff maintains firm boundaries regarding acceptable behavior; if unacceptable behavior continues, the person responsible for it is required to leave for a period of time. Anyone who is asked to leave is ultimately welcomed back after a formal conflict resolution process, which includes telling their truth about the incident and contributing to a mutually agreed-upon solution that involves forgiveness and a willingness to change. They get to start anew.

Sisters also welcomes people recently released from prison into its midst. Genny says:

> We recognize they have done their time, honor that some of their misdeeds are crimes of desperation that the city of Portland outlaws, and offer them tender mercy and opportunity. They and any of our customers can apply for positions and be hired as paid staff for Sisters of the Road.

Sometimes, when exposed to this spirit, staff and volunteers experience their own conversions, as Mary Kay McDermott recalls:

As I looked around, I first spotted Sisters' African American, tall, muscular, overly jovial, once-homeless, once-jailed cashier. He was taking orders patiently while making sure to check in with each customer about their current state of well-being as he always does. I remembered my first encounter with him — being a small-town country girl from Iowa, I was more than a little timid talking to a black man who had been jailed and homeless not all that long ago.[14]

As Mary Kay came to know this man as a person rather than a stereotype, she also came to know the necessity of forgiveness and of welcoming him back into society.

CLARENA TOLSON HAS LEARNED THE IMPORTANCE of forgiveness for breaking the cycle of violence. For example, she, like Genny Nelson at Sisters of the Road, has faced the question of whether to hire applicants who have a criminal record:

> I've had to make decisions about hiring people who are ex-offenders, and trying to determine what was the best fit for them and what was right for the city, right for our citizens. And sometimes if you put on your business hat, the easy way out is to avoid conflict and a situation that's going to cause you to have to justify yourself. But then at the same time, you've got to be able to live with yourself at the end of the day.

At the end of the day, Clarena has decided that if she can sleep well with a decision, it's probably a good decision; decisions that keep her awake need to be reexamined. Believing in the power of forgiveness, she has hired people who, after providing her with sufficient evidence that they are turning their lives around, have disclosed to her that they committed murder or some other heinous crime in the past. Her decisions have proven to be good ones, helping to give new hires a fresh start and serving the citizens of Philadelphia well.

Clarena has also seen the power of forgiveness in her day-to-day interactions with difficult colleagues. For example, a woman with some oversight for Clarena's department was regarded by many as maintaining a reign of terror. At first, Clarena shared this opinion: "My initial thoughts were just to be disgruntled like everybody else, and proclaim that person as bad, that they're just a mean person."

But she moved beyond her initial inclination and began to pray for the woman. Clarena prayed for her health and for her family and for whatever her needs were. She prayed that the woman would feel better about herself and feel better about the work she did. As she prayed, Clarena found herself able to forgive the woman for the hurts she had inflicted. She discovered that, through forgiveness, she was able to maintain an open heart in meetings. As a result, the woman softened toward her, and the two were able to accomplish the tasks they needed to accomplish. Through prayer and forgiveness, Clarena came to see this woman differently, "as a person I needed to respect, a person who had issues and concerns just like me." Clarena had done her part in breaking the cycle of violence in the workplace, through forgiveness.

Conclusion

Even if it never comes to blows or bullets, leaders must invariably face their own inner violence and that of the people around them when anger fuels action and reaction. The natural response in those situations is to fight or flee, but soulful leaders may blaze a constructive third way out of the conflict. This is accomplished not by taking sides but by staying centered while thoughtfully inserting themselves into the conflict, intervening by being a reflective or prayerful presence. The goal of this intervention is not to dampen or smother the conflict, but to break the cycle by which violent conflicts naturally escalate. Breaking the cycle in this fashion opens the way for forgiveness, respect, and shared values, the "better angels of our nature," to rise in the conflicting parties, encouraging them to seek creative solutions together.

Being in the middle of conflict, whether physical, emotional, or intellectual, takes its toll in stress, fear, and despair. Leaders faced with violence, whether bullying, threats, or dominating behavior, need to draw on their deepest spiritual resources to stay centered in these situations and rely on their everyday spiritual practices to restore them from the virtual or literal blows they absorb in the name of love. These resources allow them to persevere from a centered place and to lead by the example of their perseverance.

Persevering to the end, as the stakes on the path of leading with soul get higher, requires that leaders learn to break the cycle of violence. Leading in very different settings, Desmond Tutu, Genny Nelson, and Clarena Tolson have all learned to see compassionately, to interrupt the cycle of violence, and to forgive. These three essential components of breaking the cycle of violence work, as these leaders have discovered, in venues large and small. In city government offices, in the homeless community, and in national and international settings, these three leaders have proven their power. Once a leader has learned how to break the cycle of violence, persevering to the end becomes an attainable goal.

Queries

1. How have you learned to see compassionately in the midst of conflict or violence?

2. How have you interrupted a cycle of conflict or violence?

3. When have you forgiven?

4. How might you be being invited to forgive now?

Chapter Eight

PERSEVERING TO THE END

C HOOSING THE PATH, staying on track, persevering to the end — leading with soul encompasses all three.[1] The leaders in this book demonstrate souls strengthened and deepened by consistently engaging in the practices delineated in the earlier chapters. But across all of the specific decisions that leaders make as they persevere in leading with soul, day in and day out, something deeper and more subtle takes place. A spiritual transformation occurs, one that transforms the leaders. How are they growing through the process of leading? How can their process of transformation be described and explained?

This chapter will draw together the themes of the earlier chapters by considering the process of spiritual transformation that occurs in leaders and in their organizations as they persevere to the end. It will also consider the body of literature on spiritual leadership,[2] identifying and addressing a missing dimension in the literature.

A growing body of literature on spiritual leadership argues that spiritual leadership is necessary for organizational effectiveness.[3] A major current focus in the study of spiritual leadership is on translating the popular literature on spiritual leadership into scholarly theories that can be tested empirically.[4] Because business and management scholars are leading the way in the scholarly study of spiritual leadership, the studies are shaped by the social scientific research methods in which those scholars have been trained. These are important studies that help bring the new scholarly field of spiritual leadership into dialogue with mainstream management scholars.

At the same time, important problems are inherent to this social scientific approach to the study of spiritual leadership. First and foremost is the "flatland" state of the social sciences, that is, the focus of social science on "what is" to the exclusion of "what could be."[5] This chapter will draw on the work of psychologist and theologian Daniel Helminiak, who addresses this problem by proposing a nested hierarchy of four "viewpoints," each of which transcends and includes the one below it.

While contemporary social science focuses solely on what is, Helminiak claims that there is also a place for a social science that concerns itself with what could be, that is, with who humans are at their best. For the purposes of the issues addressed in this chapter, Helminiak's first two "viewpoints" are most relevant. The first viewpoint, the positivist, describes what is. The scholarly social scientific studies of spiritual leadership that opened this chapter (see note 3) fall into this category. Helminiak does not disparage the positivist viewpoint; on the contrary he affirms it for what it contributes.

At the same time, Helminiak believes that the positivist viewpoint leaves important questions unaddressed. To address these questions, he builds on the work of philosopher, methodologist, and theologian Bernard Lonergan and introduces a philosophic viewpoint:

> The philosopher is the seeker of wisdom, committed to the true, the good, and the beautiful. So concern for things human in terms of whether they are true or false and good or evil is called "philosophic."

Another way of speaking about philosophic concern is to speak of *authenticity.* For Lonergan, authenticity implies ongoing personal commitment to openness, questioning, honesty, and good will across the board. In this sense, commitment to authenticity is exactly what characterizes the philosophic viewpoint.[6]

By introducing the philosophic viewpoint, Helminiak is seeking to make the social sciences deeper and richer. This viewpoint is particularly important for the study of spiritual leadership. The dimension added by the philosophic viewpoint allows discussion of the true and the good. It also allows discussion of spiritual development and its normative unfolding.

This chapter will begin to fill in the missing dimension in spiritual leadership studies by making a contribution within the philosophic viewpoint. The academic literature cited at the beginning of this chapter, grounded in the "what is" approach to social science, has made and will continue to make important contributions. At the same time, the study of spiritual leadership can be deepened and enriched by moving to the philosophic viewpoint and drawing on the extensive and multifaceted literature on spiritual development.

In the field of spirituality, many studies have been done on the spiritual transformation of individuals. For example, James Fowler,[7] Walter Conn,[8] Mary Frohlich,[9] and Elizabeth Liebert[10] have integrated Western psychology and Christian faith in their studies of spiritual transformation. Gerald May[11] has provided a contemplative approach. Ken Wilber,[12] Jack Engler, and Daniel Brown;[13] and Jack Kornfield[14] have outlined the process of spiritual transformation from an Eastern perspective. And various scholars writing in the last hundred years, such as Evelyn Underhill,[15] William James,[16] Aldous Huxley,[17] Stephen Katz,[18] James R. Price,[19] and Janet Ruffing[20] have done cross-cultural studies of mysticism, outlining the process of spiritual transformation from the mystic's perspective. These are merely examples of studies done by scholars — the list could be vastly expanded by adding descriptions of spiritual transformation by great spiritual teachers through the ages, such as Moses, the Buddha, Jesus, Rumi, Teresa of Ávila, the Ba'al Shem Tov, Gandhi, Howard Thurman, Thich Nhat Hanh, Pema Chodron, Mother Teresa, and many others.

This chapter will use the classic Christian formulation of *the three ways* to describe the process of spiritual transformation, a formulation developed from the third through the sixteenth centuries,[21] which has continued to resonate with spiritual teachers to this day.[22] While the three ways express the spiritual journey in Christian language, other traditions outline a similar process.[23] The theistic language used in this chapter could just as easily be translated to the language of another tradition to express the process of spiritual transformation from that tradition's perspective. Whereas the three ways and other formulations focus on the individual's spiritual growth, this chapter will apply the formulation specifically to leaders in their context, and then extend it to organizational transformation. Like most descriptions of the spiritual life, the three ways grew out of the experience of those who had committed themselves to a life of prayer — celibate monks and nuns living, to a greater or lesser extent, apart from the world of commerce and family life. This chapter will translate the language of the three ways into the language of contemporary business and organizational life.[24]

The three ways — the purgative way, the illuminative way, and the unitive way — describe the journey of the spiritual sojourner from an initial spiritual awakening through many ups and downs all the way to union with God. While the ways, along with the transitions between them, are usually presented as a linear progression, most writers admit that even the most advanced sojourners will occasionally find themselves back in the first stage, and that no one attains union with God permanently in this life. Consequently, this chapter will outline growth in the spiritual life as a spiral rather than a linear progression.

The Individual Leader's Spiritual Transformation

The purgative way begins when the seeker awakens to an awareness of spiritual reality. Here the seeker discovers that God is a God who gives good gifts, and that following a spiritual path brings an added dimension to life. Here, too, one begins to discover one's addictions and attachments and, with God's help, takes the first halting steps toward letting go of them. In the purgative way, one experiences the bounty of God's gifts and learns to seek God for the gifts God bestows.

After a time, sojourners discover that the abundant gifts they have been receiving from God dry up. This brings confusion, as they miss the closeness to God and the answers to prayer that they grew accustomed to experiencing. At this point, they question what they are doing wrong and redouble their efforts, only to experience more dryness and frustration. Some give up on the spiritual life at this point, concluding that they are not cut out for it or, worse, that they had merely imagined it. Spiritual writers refer to this period as the "first dark night" or the "dark night of the senses," referring to the sense of darkness and confusion that sojourners experience when God's gifts in response to prayer disappear.

Those who persevere move into the illuminative way. Here they learn that the spiritual journey, rather than being about getting gifts from a gift-giving God, is about their own transformation. Instead of doing all the talking in prayer, telling God what they want, they learn to listen more. They learn to let God shape their prayers. This is the beginning of the second half of the spiritual journey.[25] Because of Western culture's focus on external rewards and on instant gratification, many in the West remain in the purgative stage and never make it through this transition to the second stage of the journey.

On the illuminative way, sojourners discover that they possess great energy to do God's work. This is the stage of good works and of the flowering of the virtues. In this stage, sojourners find it easier to persevere through tribulations, not giving in to discouragement as readily as they did before. Liberty and love characterize the illuminative way: liberty from old attachments and love toward all. Love wells up toward those in need and toward one's various neighbors, despite their defects.

Eventually the sojourner who continues on the illuminative way may enter the "second dark night," a "dark night of the soul." Here, not only do his familiar approaches to prayer no longer work, but even God seems to have disappeared. Even when the person lets go of his old form of prayer and opens himself to listen for something new, there doesn't seem to be any new path opening to God. It is at this time that he learns to desire God for God's self, not only for what God can give him. This may be hard to understand, especially if his desires have been reshaped so much that what he desires is his own spiritual transformation. John of the Cross, the sixteenth-century Spanish mystic who did the most to teach spiritual sojourners about the dark night of the soul, emphasizes that God is still at work during the dark night.[26] Although to the sojourner it appears that nothing is happening and that God has abandoned him, God is working in hidden ways.

In time, the dark night of the soul yields to the unitive way. Here the hidden work that occurred during the dark night is revealed, and the soul experiences union with God. This is the point at which the sojourner's ego and her very life become relativized to a higher good, and she is able to fully let go. Spiritual teachers sometimes refer to this letting go as "surrender." As Walter Conn puts it:

Properly understood, one surrenders not oneself or one's personal moral autonomy, but one's illusion of absolute autonomy. But such total surrender is possible only for the person who has totally fallen-in-love with a mysterious, uncomprehended God, for the person who has been grasped by an other-worldly love and completely transformed into a being-in-love.[27]

Of course, most believers glimpse this place and live in it briefly, then slip back into a more ego-centered place. Over time, as they continue to walk the spiritual path, they can learn to live more and more fully in this place of letting go. Leaders who live predominantly in this place are more available to the needs of the people they serve, and more available to their organizations. Because their egos have been relativized to the higher good, they can use their skills and energies to serve the good of their organizations as a whole rather than using them to fill their own ego needs.

The chart on the following page summarizes this three-fold path, which goes deeper into God (and hence downward in the chart) with each subsequent step. Because no one arrives once and for all at the unitive stage, the chart is merely schematic. In reality, the process is much more like a spiral (as shown in the second chart), going deeper each time the sojourner travels around the cycle again.

Because most of the focus in the literature on spiritual leadership has been on the first half of the journey,[28] leaders know little about what is occurring within them when they begin to experience the stormy rumblings that signify the invitation to the second half. Furthermore, they know very little about how to help their organizations move on to the second half.

For this reason, leaders need to understand the second half of the journey as well as the first half, and they need to know how to accompany their organizations through the second half as well as the first. How can the second half be understood and articulated for leaders and their organizations? How can leaders become skilled practitioners, helping their organizations through the second half?

To answer these questions, the next section will consider Tom's of Maine, introduced in chapter 1, as an illustrative case, with particular focus on the second half of its journey of transformation.

The Leader's Three-fold Path

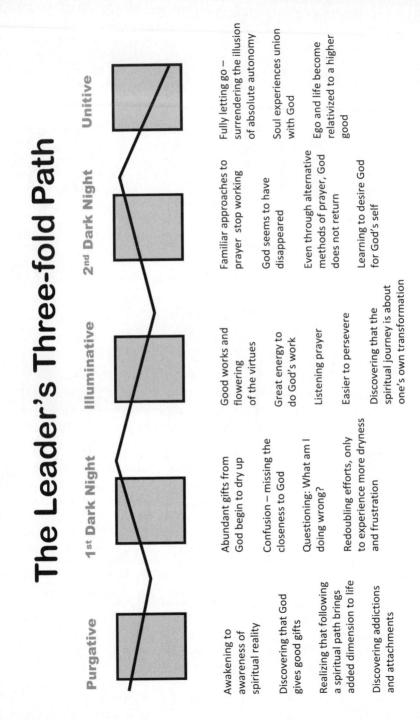

Purgative	1st Dark Night	Illuminative	2nd Dark Night	Unitive
Awakening to awareness of spiritual reality	Abundant gifts from God begin to dry up	Good works and flowering of the virtues	Familiar approaches to prayer stop working	Fully letting go – surrendering the illusion of absolute autonomy
Discovering that God gives good gifts	Confusion – missing the closeness to God	Great energy to do God's work	God seems to have disappeared	Soul experiences union with God
Realizing that following a spiritual path brings added dimension to life	Questioning: What am I doing wrong?	Listening prayer	Even through alternative methods of prayer, God does not return	Ego and life become relativized to a higher good
Discovering addictions and attachments	Redoubling efforts, only to experience more dryness and frustration	Easier to persevere	Learning to desire God for God's self	
		Discovering that the spiritual journey is about one's own transformation		

The Leader's Three-fold Path

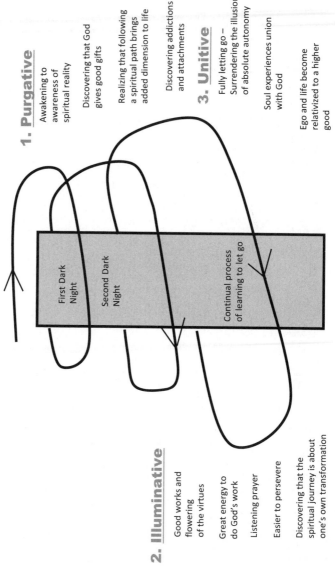

1. Purgative

Awakening to awareness of spiritual reality

Discovering that God gives good gifts

Realizing that following a spiritual path brings added dimension to life

Discovering addictions and attachments

3. Unitive

Fully letting go – Surrendering the illusion of absolute autonomy

Soul experiences union with God

Ego and life become relativized to a higher good

First Dark Night

Second Dark Night

Continual process of learning to let go

2. Illuminative

Good works and flowering of the virtues

Great energy to do God's work

Listening prayer

Easier to persevere

Discovering that the spiritual journey is about one's own transformation

Organizational Transformation

Organizations, like individuals, undergo spiritual transformation. In this section we will examine organizational transformation in its consideration of Tom's of Maine, outlining how Tom and Kate Chappell and the business as a whole followed the threefold path of transformation.

As noted in chapter 1, Tom's of Maine, founded in 1970, manufactures personal care products. In 1968, Tom Chappell was enjoying a successful insurance career in the greater Philadelphia area. Feeling that something was missing, however, he and his wife, Kate, uprooted their young family and drove to Maine, with only a dream and a prayer, to seek a new direction.

During the company's first decade, Tom and Kate traveled the path of the purgative way. In founding their company, they chose a spiritual path, putting their values first and facing many serious challenges along the way. By adhering to their spiritual principles, Tom and Kate overcame the initial challenge of developing products on a shoestring budget and finding employees appropriate for their atypical business. The early years served as the purgative way, strengthening Tom and Kate as they stuck with their values through thick and thin. By 1981, they boasted a strong workforce, a successful product (Tom's of Maine toothpaste), and a loyal customer base. Morale was high, they were giving back to the community, and they were financially successful. In just ten years, the business had grown from a dream in Tom and Kate's hearts to a $1.5 million company. Tom and Kate knew the gifts that can be realized by following a spiritual path.

By 1981, they were poised to take the company even further. They realized that they could expand beyond the health food stores where they had been selling their toothpaste, to supermarkets and drugstore chains. Hiring marketing and finance experts to help them, in the early 1980s they made the transition from a small entrepreneurial business to a midsized company, aggressively competing with large corporations for market share.

But by 1986, Tom had hit a wall. Though the company had made headway in its efforts at expansion, was beginning to capture market share, and was thriving financially, Tom was unhappy. Although he was outwardly successful, he felt miserable inside. Conflicts kept arising with the company's marketing and finance experts. They argued that nonnatural, better-tasting ingredients would help the toothpaste sell better in the new markets. They argued for less costly, nonrecyclable packaging. They said that Tom and Kate treated their customers too well, that they should cut corners more. They told Tom that he needed to let go of some of his principles if he wanted to succeed in this new expansion phase.

The old way wasn't working anymore. Tom and Kate wondered if indeed they did need to give up on their principles to achieve business success. Perhaps the principles had served a small entrepreneurial company well but hindered growth to the next level. Perhaps they needed to get out of business altogether. Was there someplace else they could go where they could live by his principles? Tom felt drawn to divinity school. Perhaps he was called to the ministry. Spiritual principles and business success no longer seemed to go together.

For Tom and Kate, this wall marked the transition phase, the "first dark night," and served as their invitation to the illuminative way, the first step on the second half of the journey. When the old ways stopped working, they could have easily given up on the spiritual path, concluding that that path was too idealistic for a growing business. Or they could have kept trying the old ways of doing things in the business, resulting in more conflict and frustration with the marketing and finance experts they had hired. Or they could have given up on expansion altogether, concluding that the business needed to stay small if it was to live by its principles.

Fortunately, Tom and Kate did none of these things. Instead they chose to deepen spiritually, eventually moving their business to the illuminative way. They realized that they couldn't figure out all the answers on their own. Not knowing where his explorations might lead but knowing that he needed to listen to his soul, Tom sought advice from a trusted spiritual advisor. He went to visit an Episcopal priest who had known him since childhood, with only one question in hand: "What is God calling us to do?"[29]

As Tom spoke to the Reverend Malcolm Eckel about the frustrations he was feeling in his business, his growing sense of emptiness, and the nudge he felt toward divinity school, Rev. Eckel cautioned, "Putting on a collar is not always the best solution in the world." From the kitchen where she was preparing lunch, Rev. Eckel's wife, Connie, interjected: "How do you know that Tom's of Maine isn't your ministry?"[30] The question bothered Tom. It muddied the waters. And it stayed with him.

At least for the immediate future, Tom and Kate decided that Tom would continue on as CEO of the business while also attending Harvard Divinity School two days a week. And in his very first class, Tom discovered part of the answer he was seeking. At divinity school, Tom found nourishment for his own soul, and he also learned to perceive and understand the soul of the business. He reclaimed the spiritual principles upon which he and Kate had founded Tom's of Maine, understanding that putting spiritual values first was the only way he could be true to himself. He learned how to articulate and develop Tom's of Maine's soul.

The wall Tom had hit in 1986 became a window into his own soul, and, unexpectedly, into the soul of the business. By putting soul first, Tom moved into the illuminative way. He regained his energy and vision. He also put the business back on course, the values-based course that he and Kate had originally charted.

Furthermore, the business flourished. "Studying theology turned out to be the best business decision I'd ever made," declares Tom in retrospect.[31] Paradoxically, when he stopped pursuing business success, business success came to him.

Tom and Kate had helped Tom's of Maine make the transition to the illuminative way and thus to the second stage of the journey, the part of the journey in which spiritual principles are put first and chosen for their own sake, rather than for the material gain they provide. And, incidentally, material gain followed.

At the same time, the journey was not without its bumps. Tom had reclaimed his soul in divinity school and discovered the company's soul. He and Kate recommitted themselves to their original values and vision. But the company's leadership still needed to be invited into the illuminative way. Tom's of Maine's culture, which during the previous decade of growth had grown into a more traditional business culture, needed to change.

Through trial and error, Tom and Kate gradually discovered how to further articulate and deepen the company's spiritual principles. The next decade proved to be a time of deepening the principles through many ups and downs, as they gradually moved the company as a whole into the illuminative way. In 1989, Tom invited his Harvard Divinity School professor Richard R. Niebuhr to lead a retreat for the Tom's of Maine leadership team. Tom believed that if the leadership could be exposed to the same philosophers and theologians to whom he had been exposed, they would catch the same vision that he and Kate had caught. In June, the leadership team gathered for a two-day retreat at a Maine resort, focusing on the philosophy of Immanuel Kant and its implications for Tom's of Maine. Tom knew that he was taking a risk by inviting hard-headed business leaders into philosophical musings. Although some entered the retreat with suspicion, gradually everyone entered into the conversation. Discussing philosophy and values was more palatable to some than to others, who wondered when the focus would return to profits. The breakthrough moment occurred when someone put together apparently opposing views and articulated the belief "We believe that the company can be financially successful, environmentally sensitive, and socially responsible."[32]

The first step had been achieved. The company's leadership was on board with values. Leaders had realized that profit, people, and the planet could be partners. The next step was to invite the whole company on board. Tom and Kate gathered the entire company in a large tent on the company grounds, seeking everyone's input on a newly drafted statement of beliefs and a mission statement, both developed from lists drafted at the leadership retreat. Though many arrived doubtful about the value of the gathering, nearly everyone participated. Incorporating the suggestions from this gathering, the two statements now read:

STATEMENT OF BELIEFS

WE BELIEVE that both human beings and nature have inherent worth and deserve our respect.

WE BELIEVE in products that are safe, effective, and made of natural ingredients.

WE BELIEVE that our company and our products are unique and worthwhile, and that we can sustain these genuine qualities with an ongoing commitment to innovation and creativity.

WE BELIEVE that we have a responsibility to cultivate the best relationships possible with our co-workers, customers, owners, agents, suppliers, and our community.

WE BELIEVE in providing employees with a safe and fulfilling work environment, and an opportunity to grow and learn.

WE BELIEVE that our company can be financially successful while behaving in a socially responsible and environmentally sensitive manner.

MISSION STATEMENT

TO SERVE our customers by providing safe, effective, innovative natural products of high quality.

TO BUILD a relationship with our customers that extends beyond product usage to include full and honest dialogue, responsiveness to feedback, and the exchange of information about products and issues.

TO RESPECT, value, and serve not only our customers, but also our co-workers, owners, agents, suppliers, and our community; to be concerned about and contribute to their well-being, and to operate with integrity so as to be deserving of their trust.

TO PROVIDE meaningful work, fair compensation, and a safe, healthy work environment that encourages openness, creativity, self-discipline, and growth.

TO ACKNOWLEDGE the value of each person's contribution to our goals, and to foster teamwork in our tasks.

TO BE DISTINCTIVE in products and policies which honor and sustain our natural world.

TO ADDRESS community concerns, in Maine and around the globe, by devoting a portion of our time, talents, and resources to the environment, human needs, the arts, and education.

TO WORK TOGETHER to contribute to the long-term value and sustainability of our company.

TO BE A PROFITABLE AND SUCCESSFUL COMPANY, while acting in a socially and environmentally responsible manner.[33]

The mission statement and the statement of beliefs had been formulated with everyone's input. But the task of living into the statements still lay ahead. Having an initial gathering to introduce the statements and invite employee input was one thing; actually living out the mission in everyday life was another. The company structure, built over the previous decade of growth, militated against it. When someone scribbled "Mission Impossible" on a pallet delivered from the factory to the warehouse, Tom knew he was in trouble.

In fits and starts, through trial and error, Tom and Kate spent the next year learning how to implement the company's mission. They learned that mission implementation is at least as hard as mission articulation. They learned that implementing the mission would extract a cost from the company. They learned that employees wait to see how seriously leadership takes the mission before wholeheartedly embracing it. Some employees even wondered if the mission was just Tom's passing midlife crisis.

The first efforts, mission implementation took place in three stages. First, Tom called a company gathering, inviting employees to take time out from their normal work day to have fun together and also to focus on mission implementation. With the help of Pearl Rutledge, a board member specializing in organizational development, an afternoon was designed to work out first steps toward living the mission. The employees enjoyed spending the day together, having fun, getting to know each other better, and reflecting on the mission. They were asked to think about how well Tom's of Maine was living out the part of its mission that focused on employees:

> To respect, value, and serve not only our customers, but also our co-workers...; to be concerned about and contribute to their well-being, and to operate with integrity so as to be deserving of their trust. To acknowledge the value of each person's contributions to our goals, and to foster teamwork in our tasks.

Tom, committed to listening, was impressed with the group's honesty. Those gathered generated a list which read:

- I'm grateful to work for a company that cares enough to listen to my needs.

- I don't feel I'm respected here.

- Tar the road—the potholes are ruining my new car.

- I'm a human being, not a human doing!

- We need a company newsletter.

- We're human, all too human.

- The building is a mess.

- We need a childcare facility.

- We need a recycling center here.

- Let's have more fun events with our families.

- How about a suggestion box for all locations?[34]

Posting the list in several company locations, Tom immediately took action on the items that could be addressed without need of delay. Painting the factory, tarring the road, authorizing a newsletter, sharing employees' childcare fees, improving safety procedures, and putting a suggestion box in place all helped to convince employees that Tom took the mission statement and their concerns seriously.

The second issue for mission implementation involved Tom's level of participation. As one who took his role seriously and wanted to do what was best for Tom's of Maine in its mission implementation struggle, Tom was surprised to learn from the company's coordinator of community life that some felt intimidated by the presence of the big boss. At her urging, Tom resigned from the mission implementation committee. Freed from their feelings of intimidation, employees elucidated their fears: fear that the mission would mean a bigger burden on them, that living the mission would be at odds with getting their jobs done, that the mission was only "Tom's mission."[35] Learning about these fears, Tom redoubled his efforts to listen and respond to employees' concerns.

As a third element in its mission implementation, Tom's of Maine began holding regular celebrations. During these events, manufacturing machines would stop for an hour while people throughout the company gathered for food and conversation to celebrate occasions such as births, retirements, birthdays, and anniversaries. These simple community-building gatherings helped employees get to know one another as individuals, and helped humanize their day-to-day interactions at work. They felt respected and valued as people.

By the end of the first year after Tom's of Maine's board had adopted its mission statement and statement of beliefs, the mission seemed to have firmly taken hold within the company.

The years that followed saw Tom and Kate and the company moving ever more deeply into living out the values they had articulated. In overcoming various challenges their values were tested again and again. Each time, despite occasional fierce debate and uncertain outcomes, they ultimately chose to stay true to their values and, in doing so, deepened their spiritual identity. They stayed the course on the illuminative way, traveling the second part of the journey.

One of these challenges concerned a Tom's of Maine product. In their commitment to all-natural ingredients, the product development team had reformulated the company's honeysuckle deodorant, adding lichen (a natural odor-fighting ingredient) and replacing propylene glycol (a petroleum product) with a vegetable-based glycerin. The new formulation was approved in pilot testing, and it went out to customers.

Within two months, angry calls and letters were pouring in. While half of the customers were pleased with the new product, half complained that the new formula stopped working for them halfway through the day. Increasing the lichen content didn't help. Stores carrying the product, and the Tom's customer service department, were overwhelmed fielding the avalanche of complaints.

The company's marketing and sales department advocated a product recall. Such a recall would cost $40,000, and would mean giving up 30 percent of projected profits for the year. They department pointed to the part of the mission statement that read:

> TO SERVE our customers by providing safe, effective, innovative natural products of high quality.

The honeysuckle deodorant reformulation didn't fit the bill. Tom's of Maine faced a moral dilemma: profits versus values. Ultimately the leadership team agreed to slow growth and reduce preplanned marketing investments in order to absorb the loss, and Tom authorized the recall.

Once again, Tom's of Maine had chosen to put values first. In the long run, the company's loss proved to be a gain, resulting in increased customer loyalty and a company reputation for integrity. But in the short run, the move seemed risky. Tom's chose to do what was right, despite the uncertain outcome of its decision.

Tom's of Maine's values were also put to the test by a major advertising campaign. Around the same time the company decided to expand its advertising, Tom got a call from renowned advertising executive Ed McCabe, who said that Tom's was just the kind of company with which he'd like to do business. The two explored the idea of a partnership, and, feeling that it was a good fit, decided to move ahead. After one false start (an ad he found condescending to customers), Tom endeavored to explain the company's values and its approach to customers more clearly. In response, the agency came up with a campaign based on the slogan "Simple Wisdom," featuring the people and the geography of Maine. Though the slogan didn't quite work for Tom, he gave the go-ahead, only to be caught up short a few weeks later when the campaign went live and a board member called to say that the ads did not reflect the company. Tom knew in his gut the board member was right, and he told Ed McCabe to pull the ads. Needless to say, the advertising agency was displeased with this decision. Realizing that the agency needed more information if they were to create ads for an unusual company like Tom's, Tom, Kate and the marketing department went to work, seeking to clarify what the company stood for. Drawing inspiration from the biblical book of Genesis and the poetry of T. S. Eliot, the team listed their objectives for a new communications strategy, which read in part:

+ To educate on product difference and company values

+ To build with our customer a sense of *shared values*, common ground

+ To convert customers to our products through awareness building, trial inducement, and reinforcement of repeat sales

+ To affirm goodness in what we make, who we are, and in others.[36]

With this list in hand, Tom went back to Ed McCabe. McCabe argued that philosophy belongs in public relations, not advertising, but Tom stood his ground. They agreed to test the objectives with focus groups, and, observing the groups' overwhelmingly positively response, McCabe agreed to try again. He asked Tom to tell him more about what the company meant by "cocreating goodness." After much more back-and-forth, McCabe's team drafted another ad:

"AND BEHOLD, IT WAS VERY GOOD..."
  You like to recycle, you like to read labels. Why are you using the same old toothpaste? What we make — a toothpaste with natural ingredients, with fluoride to clean teeth and prevent cavities — is as important as what we believe: that a company can be successful and responsible to the earth and its people.[37]

This time Tom felt that the agency really "got it," and the ad ran.

Once again, Tom and Kate had stood firm, upholding their values. It would have been easy to give in to the advice of an advertising expert, or even to give up on the campaign altogether, concluding that a company as different as Tom's of Maine couldn't be accurately represented by a Madison Avenue advertising agency. But, to their credit, both Tom and Ed persisted and collaborated until they came up with a campaign that worked. In the process, Tom and Kate continued to work on articulating their values, and the result was something no one could have predicted.

For Tom's of Maine, the years from 1989 to 1996 had proven to be years of deepening in the illuminative way and at the same time growing as a business. The company had made the transition to the second part of the journey and continued to experience ongoing transformation over the years. Then, in 1996, Tom and Kate, and the company as a whole, encountered an opportunity to move to the unitive way, the deepest level of transformation. But first they had to go through the "second dark night," the "dark night of the soul."

Dark Night

In 1996, Tom's of Maine entered a dark night of the soul. Just as an individual leader can enter a dark night, so too can an organization. The years from 1992 to 1996 had wearied Tom and Kate. The costly 1992 product recall had taken its toll: though the company had made a steady recovery from the $400,000 recall and the associated loss in sales, the recovery came at a price. Concerns about financial recovery had spurred managers once again to question Tom and Kate's focus on values. Internal politics intensified. Tom and Kate had let some people go. Tom had spent a large portion of his time on the road, trying to recapture the $2 million in sales lost in the deodorant fiasco. Tom's of Maine's best-selling product, its baking soda toothpaste, was successfully imitated by competitors, further jeopardizing sales.

Furthermore, as a midsized company, Tom's of Maine now needed a different kind of leadership than it had needed as a small entrepreneurial company. After nearly twenty-five years of growth, the company had stagnated. Tom's of Maine had lost its creative edge. In three years, no new products had been produced. The company's fifteen-person product development team, consisting of one scientist, one marketing expert, and several R & D experts, kept canceling itself out. Tom characterized the team as, "More politics than products."[38]

Tom and Kate couldn't grow the company alone. And the managers didn't have the vision to take the company to the next level.

Working with an outside facilitator, Tom and Kate called a family meeting to determine the family's involvement in the next chapter of the company's life. As each of their five children shared his or her dreams, it became clear that, while the company played an important role in each one's life and while a few wanted part-time or short-term work with the company over the next several years, each had another primary dream. None viewed the company as a long-term career. Furthermore, Kate had been developing her gifts in painting and poetry and realized that she wanted to do this work full-time. To everyone's surprise, including his own, Tom himself admitted that he felt more drawn to teaching and writing than to running the company. No one in the family had the energy to take the company to the next level.

In considering the outcome of the family meeting and all the other things happening at Tom's of Maine, Tom and Kate decided to explore selling the company. They wanted a partner who could take the company to the next level, a partner who had the vision, energy, and resources to do what they couldn't do. In the past, bigger companies had expressed interest in buying Tom's of Maine, and they felt hopeful that they could find a partner who would carry on their vision. The two were aboveboard in their communication with employees, letting them know that they were considering selling the company. They also clarified to prospective buyers and to their employees that they would sell only if: (1) the company remained in Maine, (2) all Tom's of Maine's employees were kept on, (3) the commitment to natural ingredients continued, and (4) animal testing continued to be eschewed.

As they continued to investigate potential buyers, however, Tom and Kate's hopes were eroded. The more they talked to prospective partners, the further their hearts sank. Buyers wanted Tom's of Maine for its brand and for its best-selling products, but none would commit to keeping the company in Maine or adhering to the company's values. If the company moved, most employees would lose their jobs. Tom and Kate realized that if they sold the company, only the brand would remain. The company would become a mere shell of what it had been.

With their hopes dashed, Tom and Kate, disheartened, could see no way forward. After twenty-five years, the soul of their business languished. Tom and Kate had exhausted all of their possibilities. They wondered if this was the end of their experiment building a business with soul. Tom and Kate as leaders and the company itself had entered a dark night of the soul.

Dawn: The Unitive Way

Despite the financial independence and freedom to pursue other interests a sale would have brought to the family, ultimately Tom and Kate decided not to sell Tom's of Maine. In the end, their values won out over the money. The process of seeking a buyer had clarified to Tom and Kate what was most important to them. Everything else was relativized to a higher good. If it meant the company would lose its values, then selling the company wasn't worth it to them. Their values were the greatest good:

> It was one of the biggest turning points of my life—and proof of a connection to something bigger than me, my family, my

company, and the global giants that wanted to buy us. Goodness had intervened. Our life's work was about to be turned over to cash, and we realized that the company had become more than a profitable enterprise: Tom's of Maine was selling values as well as toothpaste, mouthwash, and other personal care products. We could not compromise our mission.[39]

With this clarification of their values came new energy. Tom and Kate returned to the company with a renewed commitment to product development. They knew they needed to make up for the unproductive past three years. To move beyond the stagnation, Tom created a new approach to product development: "acorns." Through use of the acorns, which replaced the cumbersome fifteen-person product development team, Tom sought to restore the entrepreneurial spirit that had generated so many new products in the early days of the company.

The three-person acorns, composed of a "champion," a scientist, and a market researcher, embraced their charge: to rapidly create new products. The champion's job was to come up with ideas for new products that aligned with the company's mission. The scientist served the vision by experimenting and coming up with ways to make the idea work. The market researcher surveyed Tom's of Maine customers to assess the market for the idea.

The new approach proved stunningly successful. In less than eighteen months, the first four acorns were able to double the number of company products. Tom and Kate formed more acorns. Within two years of the formation of the first acorn, the number of products had gone from 27 to 117, a 300 percent increase. The company that had been languishing experienced new birth.[40]

Tom and Kate also knew the company needed a COO, someone to partner with Tom to take the company to the next level. But finding somebody who could partner with Tom seemed impossible for two reasons. First, would Tom really be able to let go of the reins and let someone else run the day-to-day operations of the company?

Entrepreneurs, notoriously bad at handing over the reins when their companies reach a size they can't manage alone, repeatedly shoot themselves in the foot trying to grow their companies, and Tom fit the entrepreneurial personality to a T. Second, Tom wanted a COO who had experience running a company *and* who shared Tom's of Maine's company values. Based on past experience, it seemed that it would be impossible to find an outsider who would fit the bill.

Tom refused to be dissuaded. First he tried a headhunting firm. Though he came close to finding someone, ultimately this route wasn't successful. But Tom continued to believe in the possibility of his dream, and one day while working pro bono for a group of Episcopal bishops at General Theological Seminary in New York, he happened upon a solution. He asked a friend of his at the seminary whether she had any ideas for a Tom's of Maine COO, and she suggested Tom O'Brien, a Proctor & Gamble executive.

When he came to interview, it was clear from the outset that Tom O'Brien "out-Tommed Tom" in his focus on the company's values. Furthermore, having served as head of the men's deodorant division of Procter & Gamble, he had excellent experience running a division of a major corporation. Perhaps most importantly, he was willing to take the risk of partnering with an entrepreneurial personality to help him take the company to the next level.

Seven months after Tom and Kate decided not the sell the company, Tom O'Brien began serving as COO of Tom's of Maine. To date, the two Toms have worked together successfully for ten years.

Through walking through the dark night of the soul, the time when Tom and Kate wondered if their values-based business vision had met its end; through clarifying their values and realizing that values had won out, that money and everything else was relativized to a higher good; through discovering new energy to revitalize the business in that process: Tom and Kate and the company entered the dawn. Their journey had reached the unitive way. The following chart represents the company's journey:

The Organizational Three-fold Path

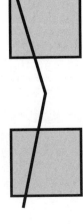

Purgative	1st Dark Night	Illuminative	2nd Dark Night	Unitive
Chose to follow a spiritual path during formative years	Transition: Can we grow and stay true to our values?	Sought spiritual direction	Internal politics intensified	Clarification of values created new energy and commitment
Adhered to spiritual principles through thick and thin	Tom felt dissatisfied	Perceived, understood, and articulated the soul of the organization	Creativity stagnated	Vision renewed
High morale, high productivity	Questioned whether principles would hinder success	Business back on values-based course to success	Leadership weary	Egos and company itself became relativized to a higher good
Financial success	Naysayers' voices get stronger	Began to move entire organization into Illuminative Way	Hit a wall: no way forward	
		Values tested through challenges		

The Organizational Three-fold Path

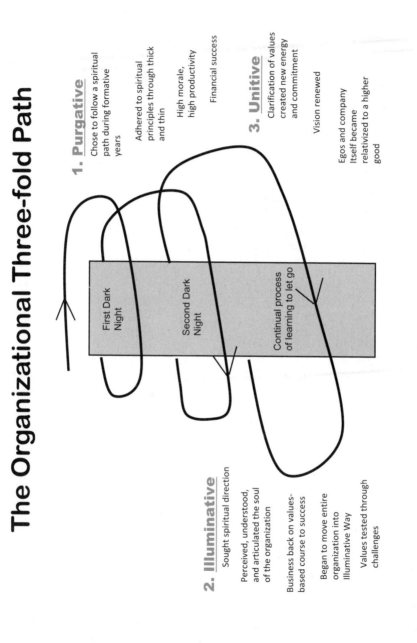

As with the individual leader's spiritual journey, the above representation is merely schematic, as the journey through the three stages with the intervening dark nights cycles around again and again. Hence, a spiral (as shown in the second chart) is a more fitting representation.

Conclusion

Tom and Kate learned to persevere to the end. They discovered that leading with soul doesn't get any easier as the journey unfolds: if anything, it gets harder. After the first decade of walking the spiritual path with their company, experiencing the purgative way and its fruits, everything seemed to go sour. By hanging in, even when Tom was ready to leave the company for the ministry, and by discovering, through wisdom gained in divinity school, that they needed to reclaim their original values, Tom and Kate and the company entered the illuminative way. After a decade of experiencing the energy and productivity that came with values alignment (the virtue, good works, and energy of the illuminative way), they entered the dark night of the soul, hitting another wall, when there seemed to be no way forward for the company to continue to grow and still remain true to its values. In the disappointment of not finding a buyer who could take the company to the next level, Tom and Kate discovered the depth of their commitment to the values. By refusing to sell to an inappropriate buyer, they themselves committed to taking the company to the next level, with the help of a yet-to-be-hired COO. The hidden work that was going on inside them during the process of seeking a buyer, the self-examination and deepening commitment to values, paralleled God's hidden, inner work in a sojourner during the dark night of the soul. When they emerged into the dawn of the unitive way, they did so with a complete surrender to the good, with a relativization of themselves and their values to the higher good. Probably because of this surrender to the higher good, Tom was able to let go of ego to a degree he hadn't before and to truly partner with Tom O'Brien as COO, a virtually unheard-of feat for a Yankee entrepreneur.[41]

THIS EXAMINATION OF TOM AND KATE CHAPPELL's and Tom's of Maine's spiritual transformation according to the three ways is a contribution to the study of spiritual leadership from Helminiak's "philosophic" viewpoint. By moving to the philosophic viewpoint, it is possible to consider spiritual development and its normative unfolding, drawing on spirituality literature and illuminating the spiritual dimension of Tom's of Maine's journey.

Queries

1. How have you experienced the stormy rumblings of transition to the second half of the journey?

2. In what ways have you moved beyond the first half of the journey to the second?

3. In what ways have you helped your organization move beyond the first part of the journey to the second?

4. In what ways have you experienced a dark night of the soul, both in your leadership role and in the organization as a whole?

Chapter Nine

FINDING SPIRITUAL GUIDANCE

L EADERS ARE OFTEN ISOLATED. Leadership can be lonely. Most leaders receive little or no training in the ways of the spiritual life. When they find themselves and their organizations going through the cycles of spiritual growth depicted in chapter 8, leaders often lack understanding about what is occurring. Fear is a normal response. Furthermore, contemporary Western leaders live in a "first part of the journey" culture. Who exists in their world, and who understands the second part of the journey and how to help them travel this path when it beckons?

Spiritual direction, a millennia-old practice in many spiritual traditions, can help leaders on the second stage of the journey.[1] Spiritual directors understand the cycles of spiritual growth. They understand the second part of the journey and can help leaders move beyond the limited understandings of the culture that surrounds them. Spiritual directors who specialize in working with leaders and organizations can be especially helpful, because they understand both the spiritual and organizational realities that leaders encounter. This chapter will provide an introduction to spiritual direction for leaders, by (1) outlining what spiritual direction is, (2) providing a brief historical overview of spiritual direction, and (3) considering spiritual direction with a special focus on leaders today and the groups they lead.

What Is Spiritual Direction?

Spiritual direction, in some ways a misnomer, is more about companionship than directing. It is a special relationship between two people that focuses on the presence of the holy in the life of the one seeking direction. Spiritual direction meetings usually occur monthly (although they can be more or less frequent), generally beginning with silent or spoken prayer followed by a sharing of what has been occurring in the directee's spiritual journey. Often punctuated by silence, spiritual direction meetings maintain a prayerful atmosphere. The spiritual director practices holy listening, listening deeply for where the Spirit is moving in the person's life, asking questions that help the directee notice and name God's presence. The spiritual director holds a memory of the directee's spiritual journey over time, honoring the reality of the spiritual dimension of life. When, in the hustle and bustle of daily life, the directee loses track of God's presence, the spiritual director remembers how God has worked in that person's life in the past and rehearses the stories of the unique ways the Spirit has been manifest in the directee's life.

Spiritual direction helps re-center the directee and reminds him or her of how to notice the Spirit's movement in everyday life. In times of confusion or dark night, spiritual direction serves as a compass, helping the directee find the path through unknown terrain. The spiritual director also serves as an experienced guide, pointing out sheer cliffs, rocky outcroppings, and dangerous crevasses along the way, and helping the directee find safe passage.[2]

While individual spiritual direction is the most common form of the practice, spiritual direction can also be done in groups. Group spiritual direction, led by a facilitator, occurs among groups of roughly six to eight people. After an initial orientation by the facilitator, participants take turns being the directee, and group members help one another notice and name the Spirit's movement in each other's lives. As with individual spiritual direction, an atmosphere of holy listening pervades the group. The facilitator provides ongoing support, helping group members hone their deep-listening skills. Group spiritual direction can be particularly effective (1) for those intimidated by individual spiritual direction who find a group experience more congenial, (2) in faith traditions that eschew hierarchy, and (3) for those sharing a common work, family, or faith experience who can benefit from joining others on a similar journey.[3]

Historical Background

Spiritual direction in the Judeo-Christian tradition has biblical roots. In their interactions with people as well as in their writings both the prophets of the Hebrew scriptures and the apostles in the New Testament offered spiritual guidance. Since spiritual direction occurs whenever one person helps another encounter the sacred, arguably many examples of spiritual direction occur in the Bible.

During the fourth century, the desert fathers and mothers of Egypt developed spiritual direction to a fine art when, after the emperor Constantine made Christianity the state religion, they fled the cities of the Roman Empire to seek a pure life dedicated to prayer in the desert. Not only did they seek spiritual direction from those more experienced in their midst, but they also offered spiritual direction to those who came to the desert from the cities seeking their guidance.

Spiritual direction as practiced by the fledgling monasteries of early medieval Europe was strongly influenced by the writings of John Cassian (d. 435), who brought the wisdom of the desert fathers and mothers to the West. While much spiritual direction in mid- to late-medieval Europe was institutionalized in the monasteries and offered only to monks and nuns by directors recognized by the official hierarchy, some spiritual directors, such as Julian of Norwich, Meister Eckhart, and Catherine of Siena, broke out of this mold. They preached that everyone could experience deep prayer and God's presence and found hordes flocking to them for spiritual direction. Because of their teaching and because many of them operated outside of the formal church hierarchy, spiritual directors like these often found themselves in conflict with the church.

Following the Protestant Reformation, formal spiritual direction continued to flourish in Roman Catholic and Eastern Orthodox circles, while Protestants and Jews tended to receive their spiritual guidance through prayer and Bible study groups. The twentieth century saw a resurgence of interest in spiritual direction among Christians and Jews alike, especially among lay people, and retreat centers offering spiritual direction and training programs for spiritual directors multiplied, a trend that has continued to the present.

Spiritual Direction with a Particular Focus on Leadership

Spiritual direction normally focuses broadly on an individual's spiritual journey, but it can also home in on a particular focus. One such type of focused spiritual direction is spiritual direction for leaders, with a particular focus on their leadership roles.[4] This type of spiritual direction can take one of several forms, and may not always look exactly like traditional spiritual direction. The following section will examine three forms of spiritual direction for leaders, providing examples for each from the lives of leaders introduced in this book: (1) individual leaders meeting with their spiritual directors for one-on-one spiritual direction, either short- or long-term, (2) leadership groups meeting with an individual spiritual director, either short- or long-term, and (3) leadership group meetings with a group for spiritual guidance, either short- or long-term.

INDIVIDUAL LEADERS MEETING ONE-TO-ONE WITH THEIR SPIRITUAL DIRECTORS, EITHER SHORT- OR LONG-TERM. An individual leader can seek spiritual direction with a focus on his or her leadership role, either short-term or long-term. For example, Tom Chappell of Tom's of Maine sought Rev. Malcolm Eckel's spiritual guidance at a time of vocational crisis. While Tom might have hoped that Eckel would direct him toward the priesthood, the spiritual guidance Eckel and his wife, Connie, offered Tom focused on his business leadership role, suggesting that God might want to work through him there. Through their guidance, Eckel and Connie helped Tom view his leadership role in the business as a ministry. Tom's experience with Rev. Eckel, a short-term example of spiritual guidance focused on the leadership role, helped him begin to reach clarity in a time of crisis.

Gus Tolson relies on his long-term relationship with a spiritual guide at his church to help him stay spiritually grounded as a leader. Not only does his individual time in prayer and reading of the Bible contribute to his leading with soul, his connection with another spiritually grounded human being whom he respects helps illuminate his leadership challenges. Through regular times of praying and discerning with a seasoned spiritual guide, Gus stays true to his soul.

Throughout his long career, Desmond Tutu has relied on his long-term relationship with a spiritual director. From the beginning of his ministerial training, he always viewed his spiritual life as central to his ministry:

> I was very blessed as I think many of us were blessed who were trained for the priesthood by a religious community.... I have always been sad that people have had secular teachers and then went on to ordination.... The community taught us, more by example than by precept, that the spiritual was utterly central in any authentic Christian existence.

For example, Tutu's assigned chore as a theological student was to clean the college chapel, and he would often happen upon members of the community at prayer there during their off-hours. Their prayerfulness made a deep impression on him.

Tutu's first spiritual director was the vice-principal of his theological college, "a wonderful member of the Community of the Resurrection, painfully shy and extraordinarily humble." He used to join the students as they did their assigned chores, "and it was very odd for us, a white man, vice-principal, who would come and work with the students, polishing the floor of the college chapel and things of that sort." His humility and prayerfulness both shaped Tutu profoundly.

In the many years since finishing his theological studies, Archbishop Tutu has always had a spiritual director. Following theological college, he sought the spiritual guidance of Sister Mary Julian, a member of the contemplative order of the Society of the Precious Blood. After her death, the new head of the spirituality department in Capetown offered him spiritual direction; after he died, the dean of Capetown became Tutu's spiritual director. Tutu chose another nun as his spiritual director when the dean of Capetown died (warning her that his three previous spiritual directors had died, so she should consider carefully whether she wanted the job!). Tutu finds that spiritual direction keeps him rooted and grounded in God through the storms and tempests of his leadership responsibilities.

In her role as co-CEO of Sophia Housing, Jean Quinn relies on her long-term relationship with a guide who understands both the spiritual journey and leadership and organizational life. As noted in chapter 6, in choosing a guide for herself in her current role, she sought someone outside of the organization, someone with a deep spiritual life, with both psychological training and a background in organizations. The spiritual direction Jean receives focuses on her role as a leader, and she finds that an integrated approach combining supervision and spiritual direction provides her with what she needs to stay spiritually grounded and to stay on top of her organizational leadership responsibilities.

LEADERSHIP GROUPS MEETING WITH AN INDIVIDUAL SPIRITUAL DIRECTOR, EITHER SHORT- OR LONG-TERM. A leadership group representing an organization can seek spiritual guidance with a focus on organizational leadership with a spiritual director, short-term or long-term. Rabbi Samuel Karff served St. Luke's Episcopal Hospital in this capacity as he met with a group of leaders from the hospital to help them design the Sacred Vocation program for their setting. He served the leadership teams of the San Jose Clinic and the Denver Harbor Clinic in this capacity as well.

LEADERSHIP GROUP MEETINGS WITH A GROUP FOR SPIRITUAL GUIDANCE, EITHER SHORT- OR LONG-TERM. A leadership group representing an organization can also seek spiritual guidance with a focus on organizational leadership with a group. Seeing Things Whole, the network of organizations mentioned in chapter 2, provides group spiritual direction, among other things, for its member organizations. By participating in the Seeing Things Whole roundtables, Tom Henry and the team at Landry's receive spiritual direction. The Seeing Things Whole mission statement outlines the challenge it seeks to address:

> To the extent that religious communities have consciously addressed themselves to organizations, most often they have been prone to our cultural ambivalence of looking at organizations either with the eyes of unquestioning trust and support or, more frequently, the perspective of cynicism and suspicion. The resulting lack of a balanced perspective which integrates both the pastoral and the prophetic significantly weakens the capacity of religious congregations to thoughtfully engage organizations and those who lead them around the role and purpose and faithful performance of organizations in today's world.[5]

As noted in chapter 2, while springing from Christian roots, Seeing Things Whole also seeks to embrace wisdom from all religious traditions. Its vision includes the following:

We are drawn by the vision of a world in which organizations measure themselves and are evaluated by others no longer on the basis of the single bottom line, but rather multiple "bottom lines," which represent concerns for the quality of life of those who work within the organization and for the ways in which the organization relates to and impacts the world around it. . . . We believe that [our] insights and learnings . . . will powerfully inform not only our understanding about organizational life and leadership, but also our understanding of faith and its relevance to today's world.[6]

Seeing Things Whole sponsors regular roundtables in the Boston area and in Minneapolis–St. Paul, as well as occasional roundtables in other geographic areas. As noted in chapter 2, the roundtables consist of representatives from four or five organizations, and each roundtable meets several times a year. At each three-and-a-half hour roundtable meeting, one member organization presents a current challenge it is facing, and the group, guided by a trained facilitator, uses the Seeing Things Whole model and process to help illuminate the challenge. Once a year, Tom Henry and the Landry's leadership team sit in the focus chair, receiving spiritual direction as a leadership group on behalf of their company. Tom and the leadership team stay in touch with the roundtable group throughout the year, attending quarterly meetings and offering their support to other member organizations. The Landry's team also gives a brief update at the end of each quarterly meeting, keeping the roundtable members apprised of their needs and inviting prayer and support. Throughout the year, the Seeing Things Whole facilitator keeps in touch with Tom and the leadership team, providing support and spiritual guidance between meetings.

Conclusion

Leaders, especially leaders who want to persevere to the end, need spiritual support. Countless leaders have bottomed out because they haven't had support systems in place to help them stay connected to their souls. Spiritual direction, in any of a number of forms, provides invaluable assistance to the leader seeking to lead with soul. No one outgrows the need for spiritual guidance. In fact, the further the leader travels on the spiritual path, the higher the stakes become, and the more support is needed, as attested to by Desmond Tutu's reliance on spiritual direction after nearly fifty years of providing leadership in his church, in his nation, and in the world. While the form spiritual direction takes will vary according to the need of the particular leader and the group that leader leads, the underlying principle remains the same: deep roots anchor strong trees.

Queries

1. In what ways have you experienced spiritual direction for your leadership role, formally or informally?

2. Consider you current leadership roles. What form of spiritual direction are you being invited into now to help you as a leader?

Conclusion

THE SOUL OF A LEADER

THE SOUL OF A LEADER faces threats from every side. In contemporary Western culture, the focus on external reality has increasingly eclipsed inner reality. Those who want to lead with soul find themselves living in a dark age that doesn't understand the need for soul in life overall, let alone in leadership.

For today's leaders, this cultural problem is magnified. Through training and subtle or explicit reinforcement on the job, leaders are encouraged to quantify the efficiency of processes, the output of workers, or their own success in management. All too easily, this concern with measurement can move into the foreground, transforming what was once a means to improvement into a sterile goal of its own. What is lost in this transformation is that which is not easily measured: the inner life of the worker or leader, the vision or mission of the organization.

Focusing on external results can be enormously valuable in forcing individuals or organizations to face realities they would rather avoid or to enable leaders and organizations to respond quickly to changes in their operating environment. At the same time, an exclusive focus on external results rules out the source of productivity and passion:

177

the inner lives and vision of individuals together with the wisdom and cohesion of the community.

When roots don't receive the nourishment they need, branches eventually wither. Long after its inner strength has begun to erode, a tree may look outwardly strong, especially to the untrained eye. It is only when a strong wind knocks down the once-mighty tree that it becomes clear to the untrained onlooker that its roots died long ago.

While this book has been about the soul of the individual leader, sometimes the focus on the individual can be a problem of its own. Particularly in Western culture, the Lone Ranger mentality of leadership is firmly embraced, a mentality that sits squarely against the wisdom of spiritual traditions. Spiritual teachers know that souls need one another in order to flourish. Leaders who long to lead with soul find themselves in inner conflict when they bump into the cultural expectation that they should solve all their problems on their own, that they shouldn't need to draw on others' support. At one level they know that they desperately need to share their problems with those with whom they can share their souls. On the other hand, they know that to admit this need will likely be interpreted by those whose opinions they value as a sign of weakness.

The soul of a leader faces threats from every side.

Yet there is hope. Leaders who yearn to lead from their souls increase in number daily. A loose network of such leaders already exists, and some of this number have already blazed the trail of soul-based leadership. In the company of these leaders, one who longs to lead with soul is not alone. Here, such a leader is not an oddity: leading with soul is natural.

It *is* possible to lead with soul. This book has showcased leaders who do it. This book has outlined how to choose the soulful path, how to stay on track, and how to persevere to the end. In each of these three phases, this book has examined both the inner and outer aspects of leading with soul. On the path of leading with soul, the inner and the outer complement one another. Partners in the dance, the inner and the outer move together, hand in hand. When she goes into a conflictual budget hearing, Clarena Tolson, for example, does the inner work of prayer before entering into her outer leadership role and finds that she is able to see with compassion and contribute toward finding a way forward that serves everyone well. She prays again after she leaves, her prayers informed by the needs of the group. Clarena's prayer grounds her for the next challenge she faces, and she grows through the process, a virtuous cycle. Tom Henry practices the outer work of gratitude by rehearsing with his leadership team all the things they outwardly appreciate about their work. In the process, he finds his own heart expanded, and he finds that the exercise shifts the team's atmosphere for the better as well. These inner shifts make it easier to practice gratitude individually and corporately, which in turn deepens the inward transformation, both individually and for the group. The process nurtures itself.

The following chart illustrates the elements occurring in this virtuous cycle, using the practice of gratitude among Tom Henry and the Landry's Bicycles team as depicted in chapter 5 as an example:

Virtuous Cycle of Gratitude (chapter 5): Tom Henry and Landry's

	Outer	*Inner*
Individual	Tom makes habit of thanking employees regularly	Tom finds his heart expanded; he develops a thankful heart
Group	Landry's team rehearses gratitude	Atmosphere in group shifts; a culture of gratitude is created

A similar chart could be created for the practices highlighted in each chapter, noting the inner and outer aspects of each practice for both the individual leader and the group, and noting the part each aspect plays in the virtuous cycle.

In addition to pointing out the inner and outer aspects of leading with soul, this book has demonstrated the process of transformation that occurs within a leader who perseveres to the end, the parallel process of transformation that occurs within that leader's organization, and the place of spiritual direction in the process. The leader who longs to lead with soul need not be discouraged, for others have gone before. And those who have gone before have provided a road map to show the way. Furthermore, the leader who desires to lead with soul has another cause for hope: help is available. Spiritual guides who know the treacherous terrain of leading with soul, the crevasses and the sheer cliffs, stand ready to assist. Their guidance is invaluable; indeed, no leader has successfully persevered to the end of the journey of leading with soul without help.

The journey of leading with soul beckons all. No matter your sphere of influence, large or small, you can lead with soul. In your family, in the workplace, in your faith community, in your neighborhood, people are hungering for leaders with soul. Take the first step; you won't be disappointed. And even more important, you will contribute something which this world desperately needs.

Queries

1. How have you seen the virtuous cycle of gratitude at work in yourself and in the group you lead? Fill out the first chart on the following page, parallel to the one above that uses Tom Henry and Landry's Bicycles in chapter 5 as an example.

2. How have you seen the virtuous cycle of other practices at work in yourself and in the group you lead? Fill out the second chart on the following page, reflecting on a practice highlighted in a chapter other than chapter 5. (For example, you could choose dreaming, chapter 3, or breaking the cycle of violence, chapter 7.)

Virtuous Cycle of Gratitude (chapter 5):
You and Your Group

	Outer	*Inner*
Individual		
Group		

Virtuous Cycle of _____ (chapter __):
You and Your Group

	Outer	*Inner*
Individual		
Group		

NOTES

Introduction / The Leader's Soul

1. See, for example, the Towers Perrin Global Workforce Study, 2007.

2. Jeffrey Pfeffer, *The Human Equation: Building Profits by Putting People First* (Boston: Harvard Business School Press, 1998).

3. See, for example, L. Davis, "Moral Judgement Development of Graduate Management Students in Two Cultures: Minnesota and Singapore," dissertation, University of Minnesota, 1987, and Faramarz Parsa and William M. Lankford, "Students' Views of Business Ethics: An Analysis," *Journal of Applied Social Psychology* 29, no. 5, 1999: 1045–57.

4. The same is true for the groundswell of books on the topic. See Patricia Aburdene, *Megatrends 2010: The Rise of Conscious Capitalism* (Charlottesville, Va.: Hampton Roads, 2005); Christine Arena, *The High-Purpose Company: The Truly Responsible — and Highly Profitable — Firms That Are Changing Business Now* (New York: Collins, 2006); Scott Cawood and Rita Bailey, *Destination Profit: Creating People-Profit Opportunities in Your Organization* (Mountain View, Calif.: Davies-Black, 2006); Richard Barrett, *Building a Values-Driven Organization: A Whole System Approach to Cultural Transformation* (Boston: Butterworth-Heinemann, 2006); David Batstone, *Saving the Corporate Soul — & (Who Knows?) Maybe Your Own: Eight Principles for Creating and Preserving Integrity and Profitability without Selling Out* (San Francisco: Jossey-Bass, 2003); Lee Bolman and Terrence Deal, *Leading with Soul: An Uncommon Journey of Spirit* San Francisco (Jossey-Bass, 2001); Alan Briskin, *The Stirring of Soul in the Workplace* (San Francisco: Berrett-Koehler, 1998); Tom Chappell, *The Soul of a Business: Managing for Profit and the Common Good*

(New York: Bantam, 1993); Dorothy Marcic, *Managing with the Wisdom of Love: Uncovering Virtue in People and Organizations* (San Francisco: Jossey-Bass, 1997); Joan Marques, Satinder Dhiman, and Richard King, *Spirituality in the Workplace: What It Is, Why It Matters, How to Make It Work for You* (Fawnskin, Calif.: Personhood Press, 2007); Ken Melrose, *Making the Grass Greener on Your Side: A CEO's Journey to Leading by Serving* (San Francisco: Berrett-Koehler, 1995); Ian Mitroff and Elizabeth Denton, *A Spiritual Audit of Corporate America: A Hard Look at Spirituality, Religion, and Values in the Workplace* (San Francisco: Jossey-Bass, 1999); Judi Neal, *Edgewalkers: People and Organizations That Take Risks, Build Bridges, and Break New Ground* (Westport, Conn.: Praeger, 2006). While such groundbreaking books as these have all raised awareness among enlightened leaders and spoken to the yearnings of myriad employees, they have yet to be mainstreamed into the typical business school curriculum or into the typical company culture.

5. Ian and Denton, *A Spiritual Audit of Corporate America,* xiv.

6. B. Alan Wallace, *The Taboo of Subjectivity: Toward a New Science of Consciousness* (New York: Oxford University Press, 2000), 4.

7. Parker J. Palmer, *Let Your Life Speak: Listening for the Voice of Vocation* (San Francisco: Jossey-Bass, 1999), 78.

8. Margaret Benefiel, "The Second Half of the Journey: Spiritual Leadership for Organizational Transformation," *Leadership Quarterly* 16 (2005): 723–47, and "Strange Bedfellows or Natural Partners? The Academic Study of Spirituality and Business," *Studies in Spirituality* 16 (2006): 273–85.

9. See, for example, Gerald G. May, *Dark Night of the Soul: A Psychiatrist Explores the Connection between Darkness and Spiritual Growth* (San Francisco: HarperSanFrancisco, 2004), 42, and Tilden Edwards, *Spiritual Director, Spiritual Companion: Guide to Tending the Soul* (New York: Paulist Press, 2001), chapter 2. Edwards points to the slipperiness of the definition of "soul" in the Hebrew and Christian scriptures, in ancient Greece, and in spiritual writers through the ages. As Edwards points out, because "soul" is "too large and too hidden to be captured by any one definition" (30), it is an evocative term that takes us to the place of intersection of the transcendent and the immanent.

10. For a further exposition of this understanding of soul and for examples, see Margaret Benefiel, *Soul at Work: Spiritual Leadership in Organizations* (New York: Seabury Books, 2005).

Chapter 1

1. Melrose is a good example of a leader who identified the "adaptive" work that needed to be done and "gave the work back to the people at a rate they could stand," in Ronald Heifetz's terminology (Heifetz, *Leadership without Easy Answers* [Cambridge, Mass.: Belknap Press of Harvard University Press, 1994], and Ronald Heifetz and Martin Linsky, *Leadership on the Line* [Boston: Harvard Business School Press, 2002]).

While Heifetz doesn't explicitly address the "soul" of leadership, many of his examples are of leaders who developed strong inner lives. In my view, one can consistently practice Heifetz's "adaptive" leadership only if one has developed a strong inner core.

2. For the full story of Toro under Ken Melrose's leadership, see Melrose's *Making the Grass Greener on Your Side: A CEO's Journey to Leading by Serving* (San Francisco: Berrett-Koehler, 1995).

3. For a more complete story of Tom's of Maine, see Tom Chappell's two books, *The Soul of a Business: Managing for Profit and the Common Good* (New York: Bantam, 1993) and *Managing Upside Down: The Seven Intentions of Values-Centered Leadership* (New York: Morrow, 1999).

Chapter 2

1. For more on Seeing Things Whole, see *www.SeeingThingsWhole.org.*

2. For Landry's core values and other information, see *www.Landrys.com* (accessed July 27, 2007).

3. See the Sacred Vocation Program website, *www.uth.tmc.edu/hhhs/sacredvocation/current.html* (accessed July 29, 2007).

Chapter 3

1. "Evaluation Notes: Aswan," *Management Sciences for Health,* September 2005.

2. Ibid.

3. "Aswan's Vision: Dream Translated into Action," *Management Sciences for Health* website, *www.msh.org/projects/mandl/6.7.html* (accessed August 2, 2007).

4. See *http://musicrising.blogspot.com/2007_08_01_archive.html* (accessed May 7, 2008).

5. Since the Institute of Medicine released its 2000 report, *To Err Is Human,* patient safety has been in the spotlight. St. John has been involved in the national movement to ensure safety.

Chapter 4

1. See the Body Shop website, *www.thebodyshopinternational.com/About+Us/Our+History/* (accessed May 7, 2008).

2. For more on shared vision, see Peter Senge, *The Fifth Discipline: The Art and Practice of the Learning Organization* (New York: Doubleday, 2006), chapter 11.

3. The Body Shop website, *www.the-body-shop.com/bodyshop/company/index.jsp?cm_re=default-_-Footer-_-About_Us* (accessed September 15, 2007).

4. David Breitkopf, "Glassman's Formula: Social Responsibility and Clean Credit," *American Banker,* November 30, 2007.

5. See the Wainwright Bank website, *www.wainwrightbank.com/html/.*

6. Ibid.

7. See the Body Shop website, *www.the-body-shop.com/bodyshop/company/index.jsp?/cm_re=default-_-Footer-_-About_Us* (accessed September 15, 2007).

8. See the Body Shop website, *www.the-body-shop.com/bodyshop/values/support_/community_trade.jsp?cmre=default-_-Footer-_-ValuesCommunityTrade* (accessed September 13, 2007).

9. Ibid.

10. Ibid.

11. *www.thebodyshopinternational.com/Values+and+Campaigns* (accessed September 14, 2007).

12. Ibid.

13. Anita Roddick has been criticized, on occasion, for not fully living up to her values. See, for example, Jon Entine, "Shattered Image," *Business Ethics* (September–October 1994), 23–28. When asked about these critiques, Roddick replied, in her books and in interviews (for example), "Obviously, we screw up occasionally; I don't claim to know what I'm doing all the time — even half the time. Beware of those who do" (*Body and Soul* [New York: Crown, 1991], 27). She pointed to the challenges of, among other things, seeking to practice fair trade, as noted above. She also pointed to the challenges of being "against animal testing," when the Body Shop relies on suppliers who procure their ingredients from various sources, who in turn procure their ingredients from various sources. Anita Roddick was a visionary who, like many visionaries, moved full speed ahead, sometimes missing details on the ground.

While the Body Shop is not above criticism, I believe that Anita Roddick's intention was to live by her values, that she learned from her mistakes, and that she achieved her goal a high percentage of the time. See also David Batstone, "Toward a Revolutionary Kindness, " *Sojourners Magazine* 32, no. 5 (September–October 2003): 36–39; Maureen Clark, "Socially Responsible Business Brawl," *The Progressive* (March 1995), 14; and Leslie Kaufman-Rosen, "Being Cruel to Be Kind," *Newsweek* (November 7, 1994), 54–58.

Chapter 5

1. "The Customer" is a trademarked program created by Ron Willingham.

Chapter 6

1. For a deeper discussion of this process, see *Soul at Work,* chapter 5.

2. For more on DMG's journey up to 2004 and its values, see *Soul at Work*, chapter 5.

Chapter 7

1. Desmond Tutu, *No Future without Forgiveness* (New York: Doubleday Image, 1999), 83.

2. For more on Genny Nelson's formative period, see *Soul at Work,* chapters 2 and 3.

3. *Quarter Century of Our Collective Humanity: Sisters of the Road, 1979–2004* (booklet produced internally by Sisters of the Road to celebrate its 25th anniversary), 17–18.

4. Ibid., 18.

5. Ibid., 4.

6. Ibid., 21.

7. Quoted in John Allen, *Rabble-Rouser for Peace* (New York: Free Press, 2006), 360–61.

8. Ibid., 361.

9. Tutu, *No Future without Forgiveness,* 174–75.

10. Quoted in Allen, *Rabble-Rouser for Peace,* 324.

11. Ibid., 357.

12. Tutu, *No Future without Forgiveness,* 86.

13. Ibid., 176–77.

14. *Quarter Century of Our Collective Humanity,* 9.

Chapter 8

1. Part of this chapter first appeared in "The Second Half of the Journey: Spiritual Leadership for Organizational Transformation," *Leadership Quarterly* 16 (2005): 723–47. Used with permission.

2. This chapter will give an overview of the literature on spiritual leadership in organizations. While a body of literature on spiritual leadership in church settings also exists, that literature is not as relevant to the focus of this book, so it will not be reviewed here.

3. R. Moxley, *Leadership and Spirit* (San Francisco: Jossey-Bass, 1999); G. Fairholm, *Capturing the Heart of Leadership* (Westport, Conn., Praeger, 1997); G. Fairholm, *Perspectives on Leadership: From the Science of Management to Its Spiritual Heart* (Westport, Conn.: Praeger, 1998); G. Fairholm, *Mastering Inner Leadership* (Westport, Conn: Quorum, 2001); W. Judge, *The Leader's Shadow: Exploring and Developing Executive Character* (Thousand Oaks, Calif.: Sage Publications, 1999; J. M. Kouzes and B. Z. Posner, *The Leadership Challenge Planner: An Action Guide to Achieving Your Personal Best* (San Francisco: Jossey-Bass, 1999; L. Ferguson, *The Path for Greatness: Work as Spiritual Service* (Victoria, B.C.: Trafford, 2000); L. Fry, "Toward a Theory of Spiritual Leadership," *Leadership Quarterly* 14 (2003): 693–727; L. Fry, "Toward a Theory of Ethical and Spiritual Well-Being and Corporate Social Responsibility through Spiritual Leadership," in *Positive Psychology in Business Ethics and Corporate Responsibility,* ed. R. Giacalone and C. Jurkiewicz (Greenwich, Conn.: Information Age Publishing, 2004), 47–83; J. Sanders, W. Hopkins, and

G. Geroy, "A Causal Assessment of the Spirituality-Leadership-Commitment Relationship," *Journal of Management, Spirituality, and Religion* 2, no. 1 (2005): 39–66; R. Barrett, *Liberating the Corporate Soul* (Newton, Mass.: Butterworth Heinemann, 1998); D. Batstone, *Saving the Corporate Soul* (San Francisco: Jossy-Bass, 2003); L. Bolman and T. Deal, *Leading with Soul* (San Francisco: Jossey-Bass, 1995); L. G. Boldt, *Zen and the Art of Making a Living* (New York: Penguin, 1992); M. Driver, "From Empty Speech to Full Speech? Reconceptualizing Spirituality in Organizations Based on a Psychoanalytically-Grounded Understanding of the Self," *Human Relations* 58, no. 9 (2005): 1091–1110; M. Driver, "A 'Spiritual Turn' in Organization Studies: Meaning Making or Meaningless," *Journal of Management, Spirituality, and Religion* 4, no. 1 (2007): 56–86; L. W. Fry, "Spiritual Leadership: State-of-the-Art and Future Directions for Theory, Research, and Practice," in *Spirituality in Business: Theory, Practice, and Future Directions,* ed. J. Biberman and L. Tischler (New York: Palgrave Macmillan, 2008); R. Greenleaf, *Servant Leadership* (New York: Paulist Press, 1977); J. Hawley, *Reawakening the Spirit at Work: The Power of Dharmic Management* (San Francisco: Berrett-Koehler, 1993); J. Jaworski, *Synchronicity: The Inner Path of Leadership* (San Francisco: Berrett-Koehler, 1996); A. L. Jue, "The Demise and Reawakening of Spirituality in Western Entrepreneurship," *Journal of Human Values* 13, no. 1 (2007): 1–11 D. W. Miller, *God at Work: The History and Promise of the Faith at Work Movement* (Oxford: Oxford University Press, 2007).

4. J. Sanders, W. Hopkins, and G. Geroy, "A Causal Assessment of the Spirituality-Leadership-Commitment Relationship," *Journal of Management, Spirituality, and Religion* 2, no. 1 (2005): 39–66; G. Fairholm, *Capturing the Heart of Leadership* (Westport, Conn., Praeger, 1997); G. Fairholm, *Perspectives on Leadership: From the Science of Management to Its Spiritual Heart* (Westport, Conn.: Praeger, 1998); G. Fairholm, *Mastering Inner Leadership* (Westport, Conn: Quorum, 2001); L. Fry, "Toward a Theory of Spiritual Leadership," *Leadership Quarterly* 14 (2003): 693–727; L. Fry, "Toward a Theory of Ethical and Spiritual Well-Being and Corporate Social Responsibility through Spiritual Leadership," in *Positive Psychology in Business Ethics and Corporate Responsibility,* ed. R. Giacalone and C. Jurkiewicz (Greenwich, Conn.: Information Age Publishing, 2004), 47–83; L. W. Fry, "Spiritual Leadership: State-of-the-Art and Future Directions for Theory, Research, and Practice," in *Spirituality in Business: Theory, Practice, and Future Directions,* ed. J. Biberman and L. Tischler (New York: Palgrave Macmillan, 2008); J. Biberman and L. Tischler, eds., *Spirituality and Business: Theory, Practice, and Future Directions* (New York: Palgrave Macmillan, 2008); V. Kinjerski and B. J. Skrypnek, "A Human Ecological Model of Spirit at Work," *Journal of Management, Spirituality, and Religion* 3, no. 3 (2006):231–41; K. Lund Dean and C. J. Fornaciari, "Empirical Research in Management, Spirituality, and Religion during Its Founding Years, *Journal of Management, Spirituality, and Religion*, 4, no. 1 (2007): 3–34.

5. For a fuller description of this problem, see Margaret Benefiel, "The Second Half of the Journey: Spiritual Leadership for Organizational Transformation," *Leadership Quarterly* 16 (2005): 723–47, and "Strange Bedfellows or Natural Partners? The Academic Study of Spirituality and Business," *Studies in Spirituality* 16 (2006): 273–85.

6. Daniel Helminiak, *The Human Core of Spirituality* (Albany, N.Y.: SUNY, 1996), 20; emphasis in original).

7. J. Fowler, *Stages of Faith* (San Francisco: Harper and Row, 1981).

8. W. Conn, *Christian Conversion: A Developmental Interpretation of Autonomy and Surrender* (Mahwah, N.J.: Paulist Press, 1986).

9. M. Frohlich, *The Intersubjectivity of the Mystic* (Atlanta: American Academy of Religion, 1994).

10. E. Liebert, *Changing Life Patterns: Adult Development in Spiritual Direction* (St. Louis: Chalice Press, 2000).

11. G. May, *Will and Spirit: A Contemplative Psychology* (San Francisco: Harper and Row, 1987).

12. K. Wilber, *The Spectrum of Consciousness* (Wheaton, Ill.: Theosophical Publishing House, 1977).

13. K. Wilber, J. Engler, and D. P. Brown, *Transformations of Consciousness: Conventional and Contemplative Perspectives on Development* (Boston: Shambhala, 1986).

14. J. Kornfield, *After the Ecstasy, the Laundry* (New York: Bantam, 2001).

15. E. Underhill, *Mysticism: A Study in the Nature and Development of Man's Spiritual Consciousness* (London: Methuen, 1911).

16. W. James, *The Varieties of Religious Experience* (New York: Modern Library, 1929).

17. A. Huxley, *The Perennial Philosophy* (New York: Harper and Brothers, 1945).

18. S. Katz, ed., *Mysticism and Philosophical Analysis* (1978), *Mysticism and Religious Traditions* (1983), and *Mysticism and Language* (1992) (New York: Oxford University Press).

19. J. R. Price, "Typologies and the Cross-cultural Analysis of Mysticism: A Critique," in *Religion and Culture: Essays in Honor of Bernard Lonergan,* ed. T. P. Fallon and P. B. Riley (Albany, N.Y.: SUNY Press, 1987), 181–90.

20. J. Ruffing, "Introduction," in *Mysticism and Social Transformation,* ed. J. Ruffing (Syracuse, N.Y.: Syracuse University Press, 2001), 1–25.

21. Originating with Origen (185–254 CE), the three ways were further developed by Pseudo-Dionysius (fifth and sixth centuries CE), Catherine of Siena (1347–80), and John of the Cross (1542–91), among others.

22. See, for example, Reginald Garrigou-Lagrange, *The Three Ways of the Spiritual Life* (London: Burns, Oates, and Washbourne, 1938); William Johnston, *Mystical Theology: The Science of Love* (London: HarperCollins, 1995); R. Thomas Richard, *The Ordinary Path to Holiness* (New York: Alba House, 2003); John J. Pasquini, *Light,*

Happiness, and Peace (New York: Alba House, 2004); Ralph Martin, *The Fulfillment of All Desire* (Steubenville, Ohio: Emmaus Road, 2006).

23. A similar process could be articulated in Buddhist terminology, for example. See B. Alan Wallace, *Contemplative Science* (New York: Columbia University Press, 2007), especially chapter 7; Ken Wilber, Jack Engler, and Daniel P. Brown, *Transformations of Consciousness: Conventional and Contemplative Perspectives on Development* (Boston: Shambhala, 1986); and Jack Kornfield, *After the Ecstasy, the Laundry* (New York: Bantam, 2001).

24. William Johnston, in *Mystical Theology: The Science of Love,* has done excellent work in transposing the three ways into contemporary Western culture, moving them beyond the walls of the monastery. This chapter will extend his work by examining the three ways in a leadership and organizational setting.

25. See also Margaret Benefiel, "The Second Half of the Journey: Spiritual Leadership for Organizational Transformation," *Leadership Quarterly* 16 (2005): 723–47, and chapter 9 in *Soul at Work* (New York: Seabury Books, 2005).

26. John of the Cross, *Ascent of Mount Carmel,* trans. Kieran Kavanaugh and Otilio Rodriguez, *The Collected Works of John of the Cross* (Washington, D.C.: ICS Publications, 1991). See also Gerald May, *Dark Night of the Soul* (San Francisco: Harper, 2004).

27. Walter Conn, *Christian Conversion: A Developmental Interpretation of Autonomy and Surrender* (Mahwah, N.J.: Paulist Press, 1986), 31.

28. Elsewhere I have referred to the work of Peter Hawkins ("The Spiritual Dimension of the Learning Organization," *Management Education and Development* 22 (1991): 172–87), and William Torbert ("Leading Organizational Transformation," in *Research in Organizational Change and Development,* vol. 3, ed. R. Woodman and W. Pasmore (Washington, D.C.: JAI Press, 1989): 83–116), both of whom make reference to the second half of the journey in leadership and organizational life, though calling it by a different name. While they have begun to explore the topic, much work remains to be done. See Margaret Benefiel, "The Second Half of the Journey: Spiritual Leadership for Organizational Transformation," *Leadership Quarterly* 16 (2005), 723–47 .

29. Tom Chappell, *The Soul of a Business* (New York: Bantam, 1993), 8.

30. Ibid.

31. Ibid., 10.

32. Ibid., 30.

33. Ibid., 32–33.

34. Ibid., 42–43.

35. Ibid., 40.

36. Ibid., 89; emphasis in original.

37. Ibid., 96.

38. Tom Chappell, *Managing Upside Down: The Seven Intentions of Values-Centered Leadership* (New York: Morrow, 1999), 20.

39. Ibid., 12.

40. Ibid., 23.

41. Tom and Kate and the company went through the cycle again almost a decade later when they were seeking a partner to take the company to a higher level. The ups and downs they experienced took them through the "dark nights"and eventually to a surprising result of selling the company to and partnering with Colgate in the spring of 2006. As of this writing, they are happy with the ways in which Colgate has honored the values of Tom's of Maine and with the ways in which the values and practices of Tom's of Maine are influencing Colgate.

Chapter 9

1. While spiritual direction, as a term, arose in the Christian tradition, parallels exist in other deep spiritual traditions. See, for example, Norvene Vest, ed., *Tending the Holy: Spiritual Direction across Traditions* (Harrisburg, Pa.: Morehouse, 2003).

2. For more on spiritual direction, see William A. Barry and William J. Connolly, *The Practice of Spiritual Direction* (San Francisco & Row, 1982); Tilden Edwards, *Spiritual Director, Spiritual Companion: Guide to Tending the Soul* (New York: Paulist Press, 2001); Margaret Guenther, *Holy Listening: The Art of Spiritual Direction* (Cambridge, Mass.: Cowley Publications, 1992); Gerald May, *Care of Mind, Care of Spirit* (San Francisco: HarperSanFrancisco, 1992); Susan Phillips, *Candlelight: Illuminating the Art of Spiritual Direction* (Harrisburg, Pa.: Morehouse, 2008); Janet Ruffing, *Spiritual Direction: Beyond the Beginnings* (Mahwah, N.J.: Paulist Press, 2000); and Norvene Vest, ed., *Still Listening: New Horizons in Spiritual Direction* (Harrisburg, Pa.: Morehouse, 2000).

3. For more on group spiritual direction, see Rose Mary Dougherty, *Group Spiritual Direction: Community for Discernment* (New York: Paulist Press, 1995), and Rose Mary Dougherty, Monica Maxon, and Lynne Smith, eds., *The Lived Experience of Group Spiritual Direction* (New York: Paulist Press, 2003).

4. See, for example, Liz Bud Ellmann, "Tending to Spirituality in the Workplace" in *The Lived Experience of Group Spiritual Direction*; Jack Mostyn, "Transforming Institutions" in *Tending the Holy: Spiritual Direction Across Traditions;* Margaret Benefiel, "Soul at Work: Spiritual Direction for Organizations," *Presence* 11, no. 3 (September 2005): 51–59; and André Delbecq, Elizabeth Liebert, Jack Mostyn, Gordan Walter, and Paul Nutt, "Discernment and Strategic Decision Making: Reflections for a Spirituality of Organizational Leadership," in *Spiritual Intelligence at Work,* ed. Moses Pava (Amsterdam and London: Elsevier, 2004), 139–74.

5. Seeing Things Whole, "Mission Statement, 2001," *www.seeingthingswhole.org/images/MissionWithCopyright.pdf* (accessed July 26, 2007).

6. Ibid.

Of Related Interest

Dave Durand
WIN THE WORLD
WITHOUT LOSING YOUR SOUL

In a culture obsessed with getting ahead at any price, many people think that the only way to succeed is to abandon your morals, cut corners, and sell your soul. But personal coach and corporate speaker Dave Durand shows us how winners from all walks of life achieve their goals — not by running away from their integrity but by embracing it. With easy to adopt skills, timely stories, and guided questions, Dave Durand shows you that:

> You have more potential than you think.
> There is a purpose behind your potential.
> You are obligated to use it.
> You can be motivated to use it!

978-0-8245-2433-3, paperback

Check your local bookstore for availability.
To order directly from the publisher,
please call 1-800-707-0670 for Customer Service
or visit our Web site at *www.cpcbooks.com.*
For catalog orders, please send your request to the address below.

THE CROSSROAD PUBLISHING COMPANY
16 Penn Plaza, Suite 1550
New York, NY 10001

crossroad